MW01174114

INTERVIEW | Joe Dante **5**
The director talks about his 1981 film **THE HOWLING**

COVER REVIEW | PURANA MANDIR **9**
The House of Ramsay, Part 3

REVIEWS | Monster Movies from Around the World! **13**
THE MUD MONSTER, **INCIDENT AT LOCH NESS**, and more!

STEVE DITKO'S MONSTER! COMIC **33**
The work of Steve Ditko and Charlton Comics' GORGO series.

Bottom of the Barrel BIGFOOT **45**
More Bigfoot Cinema coverage!

Louis Paul's Creature Feature **49**
MR. VAMPIRE, **EROTIC GHOST STORY**, & more!

An Afternoon's Obsession **55**
STORAGE 24, **BAD MILO**, **CONTRACTED** and other
monster movies to fill your weekend void.

MONSTER #4 Movie Checklist **65**
Information on where to find the films discussed in this
issue of MONSTER!

Art work: Denis St. John (pages 3, 6, and 40)

Timothy Paxton, Founder, Editor, Design, etc.
Steve Fenton, Co-Editor
Tony Strauss, Proof Master
Brian Harris, El Publisher de Grand Poobah

Volume 4 / Issue #4 / April 2014 / 1st Printing

I

EDITORIALIZING

I've been scribbling about monsters for as long as I can remember. I have favorites that inhabit the immense monsterdom canon, and I get pretty picky as to the whys and what-fors. Anything reptilian or blobular were (and still are) a given. Images of lizard men, Godzilla, Quatermass globs, The Creature, and robots (quasi-monsters) littered just about every scrap of paper I could get my hands on (including my homework, much to the chagrin of my teachers: "Tim Paxton, you will never amount to anything if you keep drawing monsters," was a statement I heard for years). There were critters that I loved and those that I put up with, and each one had a particular set of rules they had to adhere to if they wanted to stay in my good graces.

Werewolves weren't high on my list of most-loved monsters. That lack of consideration manifested after spending time with their films by way of television and reading about them in issues of various movie magazines. I found most of the monsters too dull and boring, at least in their furry form. The concept of a human being tormented by an inner beast was a fascinating one for me, but very few films seemed to make the creature out to be anything more than a two-legged bear/dog thing. To say the least, I wasn't too fond of the Universal "Wolfman", although his appearance in Erle Kenton's under-appreciated **HOUSE OF DRACULA** (1945) found the tormented soul of Larry Talbot at his most interesting. And don't get me started on how **FRANKENSTEIN MEETS THE WOLFMAN** (1943) pretty much ruined that title's latter monster for me as a kid (I'll touch on that in a later issue).

After devouring old books on the creatures by authors Sabine Baring-Gould and Montague Summers, I wanted something more than mindless beasts. The Wolfman and his kin needed to be fully lupine-like; these things should be intelligent, with a biology not ruled by the cycles of the moon. Despite attempting to stick with my list of what makes a monster, there were a few Wolfman movies that I appreciated as a tween. John Brahm's **THE UNDYING MONSTER** (1942) featured a Scottish family plagued by a form of hereditary lycanthropism. I thought that was kind of neat. Fred Sears' **THE WEREWOLF** (1956) was a fun distraction from the usual "made-wolf-by-the-moon" gypsy nonsense. In this film, two meddling scientists transform a drifter into titular monster by injecting him with a serum. Gene Fowler's **I WAS A TEENAGE WEREWOLF** (1957) went a similar route when a meddling psychiatrist injects a troubled teen with a—you guessed it!—special serum and transforms the kid into a werewolf through deep regressive hypnosis.

From what I knew at the time, most of the films throughout the '60s and '70s featured your usual Hollywood-bred werewolves. These were mildly

entertaining productions, but they rarely made any "monster sense" to me. I read about the Paul Naschy werewolf films, but they never appeared on TV or played at local theaters or drive-ins I could get to. Had I seen them, I don't think my opinion would have changed (despite all the lush nudity). Werewolf films were essentially dead to me as an art form.

Other films were made. Some of them are great tales of lycanthropism: like **WEREWOLF OF LONDON** (1931, D: Stuart Walker), **THE CURSE OF THE WEREWOLF** (1961, D: Terence Fisher), **AN AMERICAN WEREWOLF IN LONDON** (1981, D: John Landis), **THE COMPANY OF WOLVES** (1985 D: Neal Jordon), and **GINGER SNAPS** (2000, D: John Fawcett). But I have only watched one werewolf film repeatedly, and that is Joe Dante's **THE HOWLING** (1981).

I once went on a date and was transformed by **THE HOWLING**. Now here was a werewolf film where the creatures met all of my expectations; I had my checklist out and ticked-off all of the requirements. Here were self-aware werewolves. They knew what they were in human form and relished the fact that they were a special breed. These creatures could transform at will (harking back to what I had read in Sabine Baring-Gould and Montague Summers treatises on the subject). And best of all... they *looked* like werewolves: not chubby and bearlike, but long-snouted, big-eared, fanged, wolf-like horrors. The scene that most resonates in my brain is when a young woman is in a doctor's office looking for files on a patient who she suspects to be a werewolf. Just as she removes the manila folder from its filing cabinet, a large-taloned furry claw plucks the folder out of her hand... the monster doesn't knock it aside like some beast, but carefully relieves the frightened woman of the document. I was ecstatic: this werewolf was *sentient*. The rest of the film followed suit. And there you have it: **THE HOWLING** is, for me, the first *true* film werewolf.

Hallelujah!

~ Tim Paxton

Well, I cannot believe that since January 2014 we've gotten out our *fourth* monthly ish already—and they've all pretty much met our loose deadline, too. Back in my 'zining "heydays" (note quotes), it would have taken me at least that many *years* to put out so many 'zines as that! It never

ceases to amaze how quickly my tireless co-ed Tim—our main manster and master designer/layout artiste nonpareil—can crank these suckers out, but still have the end result looking so myghty *F-I-I-I-NE*! And in the space of four issues, we've roughly increased our page-count by an average of 20 pages too (for logistical reasons, we try to keep the grand total at somewhere between 60 to 70 pages, if doable). While *Weng's Chop* is undoubtedly meatier in overall size, *Monster!*—if by no means mightier—can proudly stand shoulder-to-shoulder beside its bodacious "big sister" as a more than substantial periodical in itself (without playing favorites, we lavish equal amounts of TLC on both publications). And we couldn't be doing it without all our valued contributors' vital input, so once again, thanks for all your help, peeps! I'm not gonna name names, because if I do and accidentally overlook someone's, it'll make me look (and feel) like a shit-heel. Suffice to say: you know who you are, and so do we! But one pertinent thing I do want to specifically mention is that, in ish #3, we somehow inadvertently misspelled the surname of British contributor Adam Carl Parker-Edmondston, if thankfully by only a single letter (as "-Edmonston" [sic]), but even that's one too many for Tony S. and I (*M!*'s scrupulously picky in-house spelling/grammar nazis)! So consider that sloppy oversight belatedly rectified!

For *M!* #4 we've compiled another glorious, goreous grab-bag of monsterrific madness that will hopefully assuage your jones for kooky kritters for another month (*Monster!* #5 and the rebirth of the full-size *Monster! International* [as #2.1], here we come!). Other than that, I've already got more than enough words in this ish, so I'm gonna shut da fuck up now and let the magazine speak for itself rather than have me state the obvious any further. Hope you like, you monster maniacs!

~ Steve Fenton

THE BESTIAL NATURE OF MAN:
Director Joe Dante looks back on his werewolf classic
'THE HOWLING'

by Greg Goodsell

While vampires have enjoyed an infusion of new blood thanks to the Twilight *series, and, as director Joe Dante says, "Zombies are the most fashionable monster of today," there was a brief moment in time when long-toothed lycanthropes, or werewolves, ruled the silver screen. Director Dante's 1981 werewolf film **THE HOWLING**, recently honored with a special, new high-definition screening at Hollywood's New Beverly Cinema on March 28 of this year, had him recalling the fond and furry feelings he had while concocting his monster gem.*

Director Joe Dante and friend.

THE HOWLING tells the story of TV news anchor Karen White (Dee Wallace, known as the mother in Steven Spielberg's **E.T.**, 1982, among many others), who is ordered by her therapist to retreat to a therapeutic resort named "The Colony" after a traumatic event with a serial killer. Once there with her husband (Christopher Stone, Wallace's then-real-life husband), the resort's many colorful characters and lectures about "returning to nature" lead up to the place's deadly secret—they're all werewolves!

THE HOWLING is notable for many things, not the least of which is giving longtime genre veteran John Carradine a substantial role in a medium-budgeted film, as well as actress Elisabeth Brooks' most sensual performance as a very sexy werewolf.

While **THE HOWLING** is very fondly remembered, it was just one of three werewolf films that were made and released that year—**AN AMERICAN WEREWOLF IN LONDON** and **WOLFEN** being the other notable two. Dante is at a loss as to an explanation.

"I'm not really sure. I remember when **SPLASH** (1984) was being made. There were a number of mermaid movies that were contemplated. **SPLASH** beat them out, so they folded up their tents and went home. In this case, there were a number of werewolf movies being made, each without the knowledge of the other. For some reason, 1981 turned out to be the 'year of the werewolf'."

5

Director Joe Dante gives acting advice to a werewolf (probabaly Jeff Shank).

As to the enduring allure of the shape-shifter, Dante notes that "It's connected with freedom. I think one of the more telling titles was **I WAS A TEENAGE WEREWOLF** (1957). It's the perfect metaphor for puberty. All of a sudden, you have all this hair sprouting all over you in places where you didn't have hair before. It's also connected with lust…it's the 'other'. It's the forbidden acts you're not supposed to do.

"It's remarkable that in researching these movies how far back these legends go. You get into the 19th Century, there's a lot of psychological mumbo-jumbo about lycanthropy and werewolves. You go back even further, there's all these stories about animals, and I think partly the reason why is that Native Americans worshipped animals, and the Egyptians, because they present a different side of power that we find difficult to relate to, which we sort of envy," Dante says.

Does the legend of the werewolf—in addition to other shape-shifting creatures in world mythology—point to the tenuous restrictions placed upon us by society? "I think it certainly is a façade. Just the history of the last 100 years, you would have to convince yourself that civilization is pretty much a façade," Dante laughs.

The original **HOWLING** has a satirical edge, with well-placed jabs at New Age movements

and psychobabble. "It was really an attempt to try to bring the picture up-to-date. Recent werewolf pictures hadn't done that well, partly because the blood was getting tired in the genre. So one way of modernizing it a little bit was trying to bring it into the 20th Century and use a lot of the modern, urban sophisticated aspects that were going on in society, instead of some 'animals on the loose' running around and killing people."

Dante then invokes another mysterious, somewhat sinister phenomenon all too well-rooted in contemporary reality: "*Est* was a big thing at the time. I don't know how well people remember est and its leader, Werner Erhard. There were these people who told others how to conduct their lives, that there were certain things that they had to do without. They couldn't go to the bathroom for long periods of time. Strangely, I had some friends who were actually into est. There was a flurry of self-improvement. Ideas that were floating around. We just tapped into it."

The use of a serial killer—who leaves outdated smiley-face stickers at the scene of his crimes—was another bizarre, welcome touch. "That was just an attempt to differentiate a little bit from the other slasher movies, the **PROM NIGHT** (1980) movies that had been coming out. In the 'Seventies, with the introduction of the ratings

6

system, filmmakers were able to show things they hadn't been able to before.

"Once the producers realized that one of the cheapest things they could do was chop-up the human body in every possible way, the screens were flooded with basically gore-murder movies. Although we wanted to tap into that, we didn't want to *be* one of them. We tried to intentionally mislead the audience into expecting they were going to see a slasher movie, so we could introduce the supernatural element into the film, which at the time was considered a little old-fashioned".

THE HOWLING is also notable for its mostly practical, in-camera special effects—not that Dante has anything against computer-generated imagery, or CGI.

"We did use a little animation in our picture. There's a love scene where two people turn into werewolves, and it's done in silhouette. It's actually cel animation, we just didn't have the capabilities back then. Of course, that would certainly be CGI today. I think there are a lot of benefits to CGI, for one thing. The techniques we used in that film would have been improved greatly with a little bit of CGI.

Spanish poster art for the film.

"If you've seen **AN AMERICAN WERE-WOLF IN PARIS** (1997), you'll see the limitations of not having a werewolf at all, just doing it entirely in the computer. You saw **LIFE OF**

Jeff Shank "special effects unit line producer" and werewolf operator from **THE HOWLING**.

PI (2012)? You can now actually have an animal that isn't really there be in a film. It's good for people who don't want to see animals mistreated on film. I can't see it not affecting our genre." Sadly, Dante prophesizes that "Pretty soon, there won't be monsters who exist on-set at all. Too bad for the actors, though, as it gives them something to look at that's staring them in the face. 'We'll put it in later'."

Computer imagery is omnipresent in filmmaking today, even in films that don't call attention to their visual effects. Dante argues, "Audiences have no idea how much CGI they're seeing in movies—simple, ordinary shots that they used to call 'matte shots', horizon filming—the sky changes color. It just doesn't stick out as a special effect. It's used immensely. I can't tell you how often it's used. You'll see these huge credits for CGI on the most mundane movies".

THE HOWLING appeared at a time when transformation scenes in horror films were especially popular, but as Dante points out, "Transformation scenes have always been popular. The greatest transformation scene is in **PINOCCHIO** (1940) where Lampwick turns into the donkey. The Frederic March version of **DR. JEKYLL AND MR. HYDE** (1932), with in-camera effects. The liquid latex and motors that allowed us to stretch faces, in ways that hadn't been done before. But of course, all that technology now is rather primitive".

What do people remember of **THE HOWL-ING**? "Perhaps it being the first of the Howling movies!" Dante laughs. "They've probably never seen the first one!

Dante is referring to the less-than-stellar, in-name-only, straight-to-video "sequels" attached to his original work: **HOWLING II: YOUR SISTER IS A WEREWOLF** (1985); **THE MARSUPIALS: THE HOWLING III** (1987); **HOWLING IV: THE ORIGINAL NIGHTMARE** (1988) **HOWLING V: THE REBIRTH** (1989); **HOWLING VI: THE FREAKS** (1991); as well as **HOWLING: NEW MOON RISING** (1995) and **THE HOWLING: REBORN** (2011).

In summation, Dante says his film is remembered chiefly for its originality, something which is usually in short supply in mainstream Hollywood.

"We tried to have a slightly different tone than most of the similar films around us. It's kind of a hip movie, and it's satirical, but in the crunch it plays itself straight. It was kind of its own movie at the time. A lot of other pictures made a lot more money, but they cost more money. It was certainly great for me, since it put me on the map. Just what studios were looking for: 'This is a successful movie that didn't cost that much to make—maybe this guy can do something for us'. It certainly led to **GREMLINS** (1984)!" Dante says.

The evolution of monster movies is a wondrous thing. It is especially true if you take into consideration cinema from all over the world, and not just those films popular in the USA. Universal Studios laid down the frame work with their classic series in the 1930s through the '50s. Monsters ran amok for no good reason other than that they were a creative convention for chaos. Speaking broadly, the old-fashioned idea of a monster inhabiting a haunted house was taken very seriously up into the '60s for the world market. The Italians and Spaniards valiantly kept the tradition alive throughout the '70s and into the '80s when many filmmakers considered it passé or even too childish to be taken seriously. That is, unless you lived in India. It seems that these old conventions will never fade from Indian cinema. Old spooky temples and mansions are still as popular today as they were when the Ramsay family made their mark in Indian Cinema starting in the 1970s. The two films covered in this issue of Monster! *are fine examples of subcontinental terror heavily influenced by New World clichés—which means they ROCK, by the way. ~ Tim Paxton*

PURANA MANDIR
(a.k.a. OLD TEMPLE, a.k.a. ANCIENT TEMPLE)

Reviewed by Brian Harris

India, 1984. D: Shyam Ramsay, Tulsi Ramsay

I often have people ask me how in the hell I can tolerate Bollywood horror films—*you know, because horror films shouldn't feature singing and dancing, right?*—and it's not really easy to explain, especially to American Slasher fans. There's no nudity, rarely any graphic gore, and more often than not, they're just sketchy remakes of so-so American horror films. Some just can't wrap their heads around how "just okay" films become outrageously entertaining when you throw in a few song and dance numbers and classic comedic mugging, but they do. They really do. Bollywood horror cinema—specifically Ramsay Bros. Productions—are one of my passions. When you watch one of their films you know you're watching a Ramsay film, like Shaw Bros. Kung Fu or Coen Bros. crime/drama.

When Mondo Macabro announced they were releasing a few volumes of Bollywood horror, I knew I had to purchase them all. It's a crying shame so few Bollywood classics—least of all horror films—have made it to the States, but Mondo Macabro, for the time those sets were in print, really did their best to broaden our horizons with a few jewels in the Ramsay's filmography. The films they released include **BANDH DARWAZA** (1990), **PURANA MANDIR**, **VEERANA** (1988), **PURANI HAVELI** (1989), **MAHAKAAL** (1993) and **TAHKHANA** (1986).

PURANA MANDIR is my favorite film from Volume One, the other film in the set being **BANDH DARWAZA**—which is a great film, as well—so I knew I had to tackle it for Tim, Steve and the *Monster!* readers.

The demonic Samri is on the prowl and the perfect opportunity presents itself to commit an atrocity when the honorable Raja Hariman Singh's beautiful daughter, Rupali, makes the mistake of wandering too far from her father's entourage. Caught in the web of the monster's supernatural glare, Samri drains Rupali's life force, leaving nothing but a husk. By this time, the Raja and his men have happened upon the crime and the subdue Samri. Though it's too late to save Rupali, Samri is put on trial and found guilty of numerous crimes of devilry; his

9

sentence is to be beheaded, his body buried and his head contained in a chest and given to the Raja to be walled up in his mansion. Before the sentence is carried out, the condemned demon swears vengeance, damning all of the Singh women to terrible deaths upon the birth of their first child.

200 years later, the Raja's descendant Thakur Ranvir Singh discovers that his daughter Suman is seeing a local named Sanjay. Insistent that Sanjay leave his daughter alone, Thakur does everything but kill the young man in an attempt to keep him away, but nothing seems to work. Finally, the defeated father explains to his daughter and her lover that there's a curse on the family and any chance at happiness is impossible. Sanjay doesn't scare easily, though, and Suman refuses to give up their love, so they both head to the family's ancient mansion in Bijapur to prove to themselves and Thakur that no evil exists in the house or plagues the family.

Suman's presence in the *haveli* awakens Samri's slumber and the mansion, the Singh family and the locals of Bijapur once again find themselves at the mercy of the demon, Samri. Oh, and there's some idiotic sub-plot involving an outlandishly goofy bandit, an old woman and an armless man. Yeah, don't bother over-thinking it, just go with it.

PURANA MANDIR isn't what some today might consider scary, but it was a huge success in India's rural theaters for the Ramsay's. In 1984, Film publicist V.P. Sathe noted in an article for *Filmfare* magazine that nearly two dozen theaters in the city of Bombay were sold out during its screening.[1] Perhaps not "scary", but it's undoubtedly thrilling and quite risqué in some sequences—one particular scene comes to mind when actress Arti Gupta (playing Suman) showers in a bathing suit, while blood cascades from the nozzle, covering her in blood as she caresses herself. The caressing wasn't as suggestive as I'm making it out to be, but the effect the sequence had on me was…ahem, greatly pleasing. Ms. Gupta is a stunning woman.

Interesting factoid: Arti would once again face Samri as a different character one year later in the Ramsay's 1985 production, **SAAMRI 3D**. Samri/Saamri was played both times by Ajay Agarwal, as well.

Everything, from the surrounding location and *haveli* (used in other Ramsay productions) to the lighting and score, creates a breathtaking experience and a wonderfully dreadful atmosphere that will keep viewers guessing. When will Samri strike? What will he kill? Who will he kill? Like all of the best Ramsay films, you get an exciting song-and-dance number or two and an outrageous sub-plot to pad the running time. Trust me, you won't mind once you get a load of the awesomeness that is…*Anand the Destroyer*! Okay, perhaps "The Destroyer" is a bit much, but Puneet Issar's Anand was a kick-ass fighting machine that gave his all during fight scenes. Dude had a physique and the swagger to pull off the Tough Guy, that's for sure. Cult cinema geeks may recognize Puneet better for his 1987 portrayal of the one and only Bollywood **SUPERMAN**! Nice.

[1] Sathe, V.P. (1984). "The Paradoxical Situation." *Filmfare*. December.

I love this film, can't get enough of it. I only hope someday we're treated to a gorgeous HD remaster, and DVD won't be its final resting place. Though the Mondo Macabro release for this film has gone out of print and currently sells for $100 and up on the after-market, you can grab this on VCD or on DVD as a triple-feature alongside **BANDH DARWAZA** and **VEERANA** for a little under a dollar. 'Course, you'll pay $25 for shipping and handling but you'll also be ordering directly from India. If you're addicted to cult cinema from around the world, you will need this film. Good luck finding it and I hope you enjoy it as much as I do!

PURANI HAVELI
(a.k.a. **ANCIENT MANSION**, a.k.a. **MANSION OF EVIL**)

Reviewed by Brian Harris

India, 1989. D: Shyam Ramsay, Tulsi Ramsay

After a long, hard drive, a married couple decide to stop and bed down for the night in an old abandoned mansion. Later that night, the husband is awakened by strange noises, which he promptly goes to investigate. Instead of some minor disturbance though, a ferocious "wild man" monster drags him away into a room and to his death. When his wife notices he's no longer present she goes in search of him, only to end up another casualty. Too late to save the couple, a mysterious old man arrives and drives the monster back with a crucifix, trapping him in a dungeon and sealing him away (hopefully) forever.

Later we're introduced to the murdered couple's orphaned daughter Anita, now the sole beneficiary of their fortune and in the custody of her greedy, conniving Uncle Kumar and Aunt Seema. When Anita isn't signing checks, she's dodging the advances of Seema's sleazy, unwed brother Vikram. Things only seem to get worse for her when Kumar withdraws a large sum of her money—half of which he pockets—and uses it to purchase some real estate…the very *haveli* his brother and sister-in-law were murdered at! No sooner than the place is purchased does the monster begin using its demonic power to animate a terrifying suit of armor to do its vile bidding. It quickly dispatches the groundskeeper, the real estate agent that sold the *haveli* and,

eventually, Anita's Uncle! Why exactly it didn't use the suit of armor to dislodge the crucifix from its prison door is anybody's guess.

Back at home, it's discovered that Anita is not only not interested in Vikram, but she's seeing a small-time photographer named Sunil. Fearing their pot at the end of the rainbow will run dry, Seema and Vikram accuse Sunil of being nothing more than a cheap gold digger, in an attempt to turn Anita against him and drive her into the arms of Vikram. Though she initially spurns Sunil's further assurances of true love for his physical safety, she gives in and agrees to see Sunil at a picnic being held at the new *haveli* purchased by her Uncle Kumar.

When the group arrives for their picnic, all hell breaks loose and one-by-one the picnic party members begin dropping like flies. The old man who incarcerated the monster warns them of impending doom should they stay any longer, but a picnic is a picnic and this party has only just begun!

PURANI HAVELI may be accused of many things by people unaccustomed to the wackiness of Bollywood cinema, but one cannot deny the occasional glimmers of entertainment throughout. In my opinion, this is one of the Ramsay's lesser productions; the fight choreography was beyond dreadful and unconvincing, all of the actors—outside of the

cool—and they are—but in my opinion, some won't find enough worthwhile about the production to revisit this clunker. It would appear the Indian masses felt the same way, as well, as it was only a few years after this that the brothers Shyam and Tulsi seem to have called it quits. While Shyam has since returned to filmmaking, directing such films as 2003's **DHUND (THE FOG** remake), **GHUTAN** (2007), **BACHAO – INSIDE BHOOT HAI...** (2010) and 2014's **NEIGHBOURS (FRIGHT NIGHT** remake), Tulsi called it quits after **MAHAKAAL** (a.k.a. **THE MONSTER**, 1993). I'm not saying they quit because of **PURANI HAVELI**, I just believe the diminishing returns on their low-budget productions as well as the public's increasingly insatiable taste for big-budget Bollywood epics was just something the Ramsay's couldn't keep up with. I'm sure those of you familiar with such films as **ENTHIRAN** (2010), **RA.ONE** (2011), **GANGS OF WASSEYPUR** (2012) and **EEGA** (2012) understand.

PURANI HAVELI ditches the Hindu symbolism and steamy sex appeal of the Indian woman featured in previous productions in favor of Christianity, almost no sexual (straight) innuendo and a surprising amount of clothing. Had the Ramsays converted by this time and gone a bit soft, or was it just a change-up to capture the Christian crowds? I can't say. I can say this though: when it comes to Mondo Macabro's Bollywood Collection Volume 2, **VEERANA** is the superior of the two films. If you're interested in seeing and owning this film despite my lukewarm "praise", *Induna.com* sells both VCDs and DVDs of this title. Have fun!

comedic relief and the old man—were stiff and boring, and the leads obviously could not dance, as they barely moved during the song and dance routines. I like the film—don't get me wrong—I just feel that the location, monster and comedic sub-plot were far better than the actual film itself. Sure, some of the gay jokes between Mangu and Sher Khan were a bit juvenile and the Mangu/Gangu sub-plot had me scratching my head, but they were pretty funny.

The horror fans may find the suit of demonic armor, the monster and the Christian trappings

REVIEWS

THE MUD MONSTER
(a.k.a. THE WORLD BEYOND)

Reviewed by Steve Fenton

USA, 1978. D: Noel Black

Ad-line: *"Condemned to fight a living nightmare"*

Produced by Time-Life Television Productions for airing on CBS, **THE MUD MONSTER**, while set in Maine, was actually shot on location, of all places, in Gananoque, near Kingston, Ontario (amidst the Thousand Islands of Lake Ontario, which is freshwater, despite this show's alleged Atlantic Ocean island milieu). Original *TV Guide* listings stated, "This is a pilot for a possible, but unscheduled, series". Under its original title **THE WORLD BEYOND**, it was intended as the lead-in to a whole supernaturally-themed series (the initial pilot which preceded it was entitled **THE WORLD OF DARKNESS** [1977]), but unfortunately it never developed further than this, which is about all we're left with, I'm afraid. There are some rudimentary plot similarities to Michael Caffey's interestingly offbeat tele-Western **THE HANGED MAN** (1974, USA), another proposed series that never went further than the pilot stage. Although that film certainly didn't contain anything even remotely resembling a monster—be it made of mud or otherwise—its main character (played by Dana Andrews' real-life kid brother Steve Forrest) was a wrongfully convicted and condemned gunslinger who, after being strung-up due to a miscarriage of justice and thereafter pronounced dead, "miraculously" returns to life, whereupon he shortly learns that, possibly due to some sort of supernatural intervention, he has since developed pronounced clairvoyant abilities. The rudiments of Forrest's character in that film can also be seen in Granville van Dusen's character here (who, despite being wholly unlike him in both looks and personality, also contains trace elements of Darren McGavin as Carl Kolchak, "The Night Stalker").

If the majority of the user reviews at IMDb are anything to go by, most of the people who saw this show as kids were scared shitless—and possibly even left scarred for life—by it. Although I did get to see a number of other horror-themed teleseries and telemovies during the same general period (including *Kolchak: The Night Stalker*

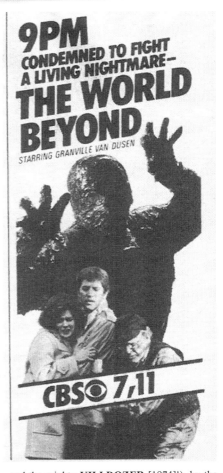

and the mighty **KILLDOZER** [1974]!), by the time the present title originally aired—it was produced in '77 and first broadcast at the end of January '78—I was already in my late teens and well-used to watching monster movies by then, so even if I had seen it it likely wouldn't have caused me to lose any sleep due to the traumatic intensity of the experience. By that point in my life, I had already seen Paul Morrissey and Antonio Margheriti's **FLESH FOR FRANKENSTEIN** (1973, USA/Italy/France), plus Morrissey's **BLOOD FOR DRACULA** (1974, Italy/France), Jeff Leiberman's calamity of worms eco-chiller **SQUIRM** (1976, USA) and David Cronenberg's shape-of-rage contagion shocker **RABID** (1977, Canada) during

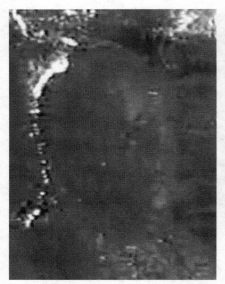

Left: His Name is Mud, the best image available of the murky "Mud Monster" and, above, Ho Meng-hua's monster classic **THE OILY MANIAC**.

their original theatrical runs…so I was ready for just about *anything* that the small screen might throw at me! Unlike now, back then the boob tube (when it largely consisted of commercial networks governed by strict broadcasting rules) was generally known as a comparatively tamer medium than the cinema; so as a lover of horror and monster movies, I didn't have very high expectations of it, for the most part.

And so, to **THE MUD MONSTER**…

Following a near-permanently-fatal motorcycle accident—for which he is left legally dead for just over 2½ minutes—a sports journalist named Paul Taylor (van Dusen) returns to life and becomes inexplicably gifted with extra sensory perception as a direct result of his more than just near-death experience. The voice of a dead person in his head dispatches him to the out-of-the-way Maine community of Logan's Island. Taylor's companion on the boat ride is Marian Faber (a pre-**POLTERGEIST** JoBeth Williams), none other than the very person he has been sent to warn about some as-yet-unknown danger both he and we can at this point only guess at… but that title ought to give us a valuable clue! In an ominous bit of foreshadowing, Borchard the boatman (special guest star Barnard Hughes [1915-2006]), who ferries Taylor and Marian to the island, is savagely bitten by his ordinarily gentle and loving she-mutt, Lover, who in addition to being a literal bitch suddenly turns into a figurative one, as well. In another eerie portent that all is not right on the isolated body of land,

in the boathouse upon their arrival Mrs. Faber's absent brother Frank's motor launch is found scuppered at the dock. Within the deserted, shuttered and boarded-up house—which appears to be barricaded specifically to keep something out—Taylor finds old books on the occult (including one entitled *Spells and Incantations*), but no sign of Marian's missing bro anywhere. Unexplainable splotches of mud are found all over the property, both within and without the house. The three stranded visitors endeavor to make it to a neighbor's—the only other residence on the island—in hopes of borrowing a boat in order to make their getaway. But something *non-human* endeavors to prevent them from leaving…

It develops that Marian Faber's brother, a dabbler in the occult sciences, had constructed a *golem* ("a body without a soul") out of the clay and sticks of the Earth, then brought the inanimate object to unnatural life using cabalist sorcery. "It's made outta mud", says van Dusen as Taylor matter-of-factly, as though it's an absolute given rather than an utter impossibility. "Mud pies don't go around killin' dogs and people!" exclaims Hughes as Borchard, who is just as openly disbelieving as Williams' Marian character. However, the excavated outline of a huge humanoid body is found in the muddy ground nearby, as though something buried there has recently unearthed itself…which indeed it has.

Great care and detail obviously went into the sound engineering on this production, and it plays a major part in establishing and maintaining the creepy ambience throughout. Even the umpteenth reuse of the old "creaking, self-slamming door" gimmick (an antiquated plot device which was already old hat even way back in 1930) doesn't spoil the mood. Extra eeriness and unease is added by a cacophony of strange, unsettling sounds heard on the audio track, coupled with "prowling-through-the-bush" POV shots of a lurking *something* which clearly isn't human. Horrifying inhuman roars seem to confirm this beyond a shadow of a doubt. So much exaggerated roaring and howling is heard coming from off-screen that I couldn't help being reminded of José Antonio Nieves Conde's nifty "invisible monster" movie **SOUND OF HORROR** (a.k.a. *El Sonido Prehistorico*, "*The Prehistoric Sound*", 1965, Spain); but, other than for the marooned cast members and all the racket the highly vocal if as-yet-unseen monster kicks up, there all similarities end.

In a quite gruesome bit of business for the time, Mr. Borchard finds the shredded, broken-necked remains of his dog (albeit merely an obvious dummy stand-in). The first real sighting we and the protagonists get of (quote) "that murderin' monster, or whatever it is"—which appears unexpectedly outside an opened door, growling menacingly—is highly reminiscent of a similar encounter between the humans and the vegetable (if by no means vegetarian) alien in Howard Hawks' **THE THING FROM ANOTHER WORLD** (1951, USA). Also rather reminiscent of that film, the golem gets one of its arms chopped-off at the elbow, whereafter hero van Dusen and heroine Williams interact with this severed forearm, which takes on a life of its own ("It was *alive!*") and makes a grab for the latter. A subsequent nerve-rattling scene comes when, while trying to get at them, the disembodied arm, having been locked in the cellar, rattles the door knob. It is while engaging in a *mano a mano* ("hand-to-hand" [pun intended]) struggle with the bodiless limb that van Dusen accidentally learns the simple but effective means of disposing of the supernatural creature made from mud. During the epilogue, some "convenient" if clumsy belated exposition helps—so they hoped!—rationalize a few gaping illogicalities/inconsistencies in the plot, but I won't go into those, because in order to do so I would have to give away the ending and spoil it for everybody…which I'm not going to do—not *this* time anyway (that makes a change)! One final minor twist I will divulge is that the mainland authorities' official report as to the perpetrator of the killings attributes them to "Person or persons unknown".

While I was hoping for some sort of Americanized variant of Ho Meng-hua's loony Hong Kong monster flick **THE OILY MANIAC** (a.k.a. 油鬼子 / *You gui zi*, 1976), possibly with a bit of Eddie Cahn's crusty **CURSE OF THE FACE-**

"Seriously, give me *any* reason to post a photo from **CURSE OF THE FACELESS MAN**, and I'm all over it!"
~ editor Tim

15

LESS MAN (1958, USA) thrown in for bad measure, what I actually got was a not-so-gentle gentile reinterpretation of the ancient "Golem" legend (Rabbi Loew of Prague from the most famous story is name-dropped, as is some mystical/theological mumbo-jumbo purportedly derived from the Kabbalah in hopes of lending a veneer of credibility to the proceedings). At a mere 49 minutes' duration, **THE MUD MONSTER** out of necessity gets where it's going without any undue wasted time. Without going overboard or causing too many lags in the pacing, there is sufficient character development to make us give more than just a hoot about the principal players, and the male and female leads manage to generate some believable chemistry, mostly playing it understated.

On strength of the material seen here, it's a shame the proposed series never went further than it did.

NOTES: Although simply because it's catchier and I like it better I've gone with the more lurid alternate title used to head this review, the actual onscreen title of the episode is simply "Monster" (now, if it had an exclamation point after it, I'd like it a lot better! [subtle in-joke alert]). While watchable enough in lieu of a better copy, the version at YouTube is appropriately enough—if annoyingly—muddy as hell, and places a thick layer of surface silt between the viewer and the action. Apparently it is (was?) available on DVD from Cinefear via such sources as the *superstrangevideo.com* website.

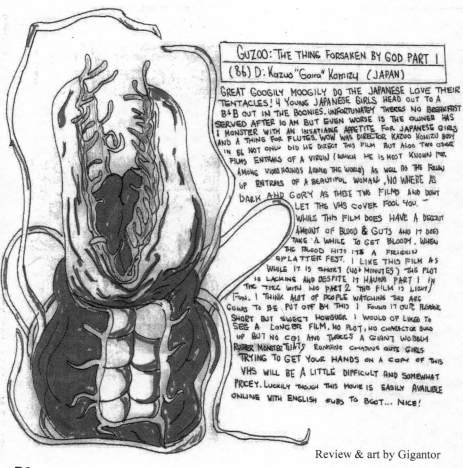

GUZOO: THE THING FORSAKEN BY GOD PART 1
(86) D: Kazuo "Gaira" Komizu (JAPAN)

GREAT GOOGILY MOOGILY DO THE JAPANESE LOVE THEIR TENTACLES! 4 YOUNG JAPANESE GIRLS HEAD OUT TO A B+B OUT IN THE BOONIES. UNFORTUNATELY THERES NO BREAKFAST SERVED AFTER 10 AM BUT EVEN WORSE IS THE OWNER HAS 1 MONSTER WITH AN INSATIABLE APPETITE FOR JAPANESE GIRLS AND A THING FOR FLUTES. WOW WAS DIRECTOR KAZUO KOMIZU BUSY IN 86 NOT ONLY DID HE DIRECT THIS FILM BUT ALSO TWO OTHER FILMS ENTRAILS OF A VIRGIN (WHICH HE IS MOST KNOWN FOR AMONG VIDEO HOUNDS AROUND THE WORLD) AS WELL AS THE FOLLOW UP ENTRAILS OF A BEAUTIFUL WOMAN, NO WHERE AS DARK AND GORY AS THESE TWO FILMS AND DONT LET THE VHS COVER FOOL YOU.

WHILE THIS FILM DOES HAVE A DECENT AMOUNT OF BLOOD & GUTS AND IT DOES TAKE A WHILE TO GET BLOODY. WHEN THE BLOOD HITS ITS A FRIGGIN SPLATTER FEST. I LIKE THIS FILM AS WHILE IT IS SHORT (40+ MINUTES) THE PLOT IS LACKING AND DESPITE IT HAVING PART 1 IN THE TITLE WITH NO PART 2 THIS FILM IS LIGHT/FUN. I THINK ALOT OF PEOPLE WATCHING THIS ARE GOING TO BE PUT OFF BY THIS. I FOUND IT OUTE PLEASE SHORT BUT SWEET HOWEVER I WOULD OF LIKED TO SEE A LONGER FILM. NO PLOT, NO CHARACTER BUILD UP BUT NO CGI AND THERES A GIANT WOBBLY RUBBER MONSTER THATS RUNNING CHASING CUTE GIRLS TRYING TO GET YOUR HANDS ON A COPY OF THIS VHS WILL BE A LITTLE DIFFICULT AND SOMEWHAT PRICEY. LUCKILY THOUGH THIS MOVIE IS EASILY AVAILIBLE ONLINE WITH ENGLISH SUBS TO BOOT... NICE!

Review & art by Gigantor

TO KAKO

Reviewed by Christos Mouroukis

Greece, 2005. D: Yorgos Noussias (Γιωργοσ Νουσιασ)

If you haven't already seen **EVIL** (the English-language release title for **TO KAKO**), imagine **28 DAYS LATER...** (2002) meets **RUN LOLA RUN** (1998)—the Greek way.

Pre-credits, three archaeologists during an expedition are attacked by an unseen evil. Soon there will be a major zombie outbreak in Central Athens, and in impressive settings such as a rave party and a football stadium. The army has no solution—the soldiers killed each other.

From then on we follow the adventures of a group of survivors, who try to...*er*, survive. Some of them will die and some will live in the midst of slaughtering, mayhem, disembowelments, exploding heads, mutilations and infections, until the nightmarish finale.

The screenplay is weak and so is the acting, but they're both very ambitious, and that's all that matters, really. The soundtrack will remind you of your favourite '80s Italian zombie epics. Also, the sound design is possibly the best I've ever heard in a Greek film. The visual effects are great (especially considering the low budget of the totally independent production) and the practical effects are even greater.

I don't remember how many years have passed, but I attended one of my films' screenings in the Fantasy Festival of Hilioupolis, and to my pleasant surprise I caught a George Alahouzos and Roulis Alahouzos Q&A along with clips from **THE EVIL**, for which they created the gory effects. Many years later I introduced myself to them at London's Greek Film Festival, and they are such nice guys. Speaking of London, I was shopping at HMV one day and I noticed DVD copies of **THE EVIL**, which made me a happy and proud genre fan, because for example, no matter how expensive Theodoros Angelopoulos "art-house" co-productions were, I've never spotted one of his films on DVD abroad.

TO KAKO had brilliant promotion. I was living in Athens when it came out and you could see posters and flyers everywhere, and as a result the film was really successful, especially with young audiences. It is, in my opinion, Greece's most important '00s genre film, because while there have been others, none have had its impact. Well done!

TO KAKO 2 - STIN EPOHI TON IROON
(a.k.a. **TO KAKÓ 2: ΣΤΗΝ ΕΠΟΧΗ ΤΩΝ ΗΡΏΩΝ**, a.k.a. **EVIL - IN THE TIME OF HEROES**)

Reviewed by Christos Mouroukis

Greece, 2009. D: Yorgos Noussias (Γιωργοσ Νουσιασ)

Okay, now we have to do with a sort of a mainstream horror/sci-fi/action film (starring Billy Zane from **TITANIC** [1997]). Following the success of the first movie, **TO KAKO** (a.k.a. **EVIL**, 2005), every respected celluloid establishment wanted to jump on board. The Greek Film Centre (Greece's public movie council) and Audio Visual (a major company), among others, actually did.

In a pre-credit sequence a zombie horde attacks a bunch of ancient Greeks. Yes, the film goes back to thousands of years ago. From then on we follow the story of a group of survivors who have to

INCIDENT AT LOCH NESS

Reviewed by Tony Strauss

UK, 2004. D: Zak Penn

This is the story of two men's struggle to achieve their respective filmmaking goals: The first man, acclaimed filmmaker Werner Herzog (brilliantly played with utter conviction and believability by acclaimed filmmaker Werner Herzog), wants to realize his goal of making a documentary about the Loch Ness region and the tales, legends and people surrounding the area; the second, Hollywood power-scribe Zak Penn (here portrayed by real-life lookalike Zak Penn, screenwriter of **BEHIND ENEMY LINES**, **SUSPECT ZERO** and **THE INCREDIBLE HULK**), wants to realize his goal of producing a Werner Herzog documentary and winning awards for doing so. On paper, the two men seem to have more-or-less the same goal—at least close enough to make this a successful pairing on a filmmaking project of this nature—but the differences in vision and method may be the death of the production…if not the entire crew.

Things start out amicably enough at the dinner party in the Herzog home which kicks off the production (including attending guests such as magician/actor Ricky Jay and actor/suave-stammerer Jeff Goldblum), until the cinematographer

fight not only zombies but also paranoid shooters who kill for fun in the midst of chaos. And if that's not enough, title cards prepare us for a bombing. Speaking of title cards, they help us to understand what's going on because the editing goes back and forth plenty of times.

We lived to see that too: a polished zombie film from Greece. It is really impressive and I dare to say that it is the best genre film to ever come out of Greece. You have to have balls to pull off something like that.

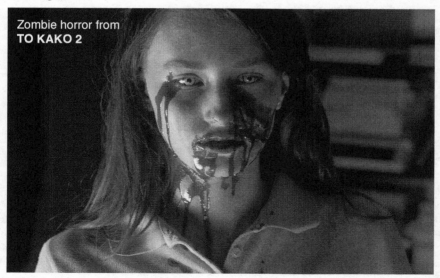

Zombie horror from
TO KAKO 2

Penn has hired, Gabriel Beristain (D.P. of such big-scale fare as **K2**, **BLOOD IN, BLOOD OUT**, and **BLADE II**) pulls Penn and Herzog aside to ask why his lighting package is so small. Herzog is baffled by the question ("Lighting package? This is a documentary."), but Penn quickly dismisses the question, promising to work it out later, and rushes the two back to the dinner party, having obviously been caught promising two different things to the two men. This seems to be an awkward though easily surmountable problem, but it turns out to be just the tip of the iceberg with regards to Penn's big Hollywood ideas and methods poisoning the well of Herzog's small-scale documentary. At the first production meeting, Penn hands out "official expedition jumpsuits" for everyone to wear during the production (with "expedition" misspelled on the back); he's hired a small local boat to take them out onto the loch, and has arbitrarily renamed the boat "Discovery IV" because he thinks it sounds cool; he's hired a bikini model to be the team's sonar operator and a crazy cryptozoologist who's fiercely protective of the Nessie legend; and despite the fact that this is supposedly a documentary about the region's legends and people, Penn has secretly hired an FX crew to build a remote-controlled practical effect...

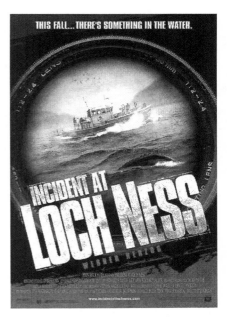

While Penn is clearly duping every member of the crew on one level or another, he maintains his self-aggrandizing attitude of the typical Hollywood autocratic producer, feeling he knows what's best for the production, and that he is in this role achieving a long-deserved and long-overdue status of power (during an interview segment, he indignantly expresses his desire to finally be the one who gets to say, "Fire *that* writer."). Meanwhile, as Herzog discovers more and more of Penn's deceptions and manipulations, he rapidly begins to regret making this one exception to his usual practice of producing his own films. As tensions increase and the production begins to break down from in-fighting and crew member abandonment, it seems that the "Discovery IV" has captured the attention of something living in the lake that is *not* a remote-controlled practical effect. The proceedings are about to evolve into a fight for survival while the production's two figureheads continue to battle for creative control. Even with his life in danger, Herzog has only one thought on his mind: "...if I survive this, I was gonna find Zak Penn, and I would hunt him down, and I would strangle him with my two hands."

Achieving maximum verisimilitude by the simple inclusion of Werner Herzog in a documen-

tary setting, this brilliantly subversive mockumentary seems to have fooled as many people as the original **THE BLAIR WITCH PROJECT** (1999), with pockets of debate over its authenticity still raging online to this day. This is a testament to how well-planned and executed a film this is; given Herzog's history of redefining the term "troubled production", it is all-too-easy to believe that this is merely a depiction of yet another Herzog production gone awry. And this is part of writer/director Penn's genius here—he creates such subtle and believable parodies of both Herzog and himself (or, more to the point, the "typical Hollywood attitude"), and introduces the satire so gradually that the suspension of disbelief sneaks up on the viewer without distraction, and allows us to be fully immersed in the proceedings as they become more and more hysterical and outlandish. At one point, Herzog angrily informs Penn, "This is the most chaotic production I've ever seen...and I've seen some big ones," to which the clearly butt-hurt Penn mutters under his breath, "At least we're not dragging the boat over a hill."[1]

While easily accessible and enjoyable to nearly any audience, a modicum of foreknowledge of Herzog's reputation and methods and how

---

[1] A reference to Herzog's famously horrific production of **FITZCARRALDO** (1982)—in which the director insisted on doing just that—which was depicted in Les Blank's harrowing behind-the-scenes documentary, **BURDEN OF DREAMS** (1982).

THE WHITE BUFFALO

Reviewed by Steve Fenton

USA, 1977. D: J. Lee Thompson

Ad-line: *"Charging... Roaring... Breathing Fire and Hell... The White Earthquake is Here!"*

Adapted from the book and script by Richard Sales, this Hollywood "monster Western" mega-flop was funded by Roman producer Dino De Laurentiis (it was released in Italy as **SFIDA A WHITE BUFFALO** / "Challenge of the White Buffalo"). In 1874, Buffalo hunter "Wild Bill" Hickok (Charles Bronson) is plagued by nightmares of a giant white bison, one of the most sacred symbols in the mythology of the American Indian. Hickok heads to stake his claim in the Black Hills, where gold has been struck smack-dab in the middle of Lakota Sioux territory. The Sioux hate Wild Bill because he was responsible for killing a great Indian leader known as Whistler, the Peacemaker.

To complicate Wild Bill's job still further, Captain Tom Custer (the buffalo-sized Clint Walker) hunts Hickok for being an alleged low-down dirty backshooter ("You're lookin' to wear a marble hat!"). Bronson's character—dubbed *Bahaska* ("longhair") by the Cheyenne—appears suitably mysterious, complete with dark glasses and assumed name (to fool the vengeful Sioux, who are regarded as little more than [quote] "red niggers" by racist whites). When it materializes, the white buffalo emits Godzilla-like roars, terrorizing and trampling Indians underhoof. Chief Crazy Horse (Native American actor Will Sampson, a regular fixture of such mystical mumbo-jumbo, who was also seen in Dino's killer whale thriller **ORCA**—another megaflop—the same year) is grief-stricken and enraged when his juvenile daughter is fatally gored by the beast. Both Crazy Horse and Wild Bill vie for the buff's hide—the former simply for revenge; the latter perhaps for even darker reasons beyond the mere $2000 cash bounty he stands to gain from the pelt.

THE WHITE BUFFALO—originating from Dino's much-derided "giant critter" production phase—seems undecided as to whether its script's beastly nemesis actually exists within the context of the narrative, or is simply a fantastical figment of Wild Bill's tormented imagination (his personal white whale...or merely a pink elephant?). Much like his obsessively driven Harmonica character in Sergio Leone's

they differ from typical big-budget Hollywood productions will multiply the viewer's enjoyment level tenfold, and have you pausing the film repeatedly until you recover from laughter. Whether you're a big mockumentary fan, a cryptozoology enthusiast, a lover of documentaries, or, most importantly, just a Herzog fan, this is an absolute must-see satire that'll still have you giggling for days afterward.

[*NOTE:* After viewing the film, be sure to listen to the director's commentary on the DVD to catch up on the hilarious "aftermath" of this disastrous production...they really follow-through on their swing with this one.]

ONCE UPON A TIME IN THE WEST (*C'era una volta il West*, 1968, Italy/USA), Bronson as Hickok—evidently channeling both Melville's whaler Cap'n Ahab and Spielberg's shark hunter Quint, each relentlessly driven characters—is convinced that his entire life thus far has merely been a prelude to his ultimate date with Destiny. At one point, the demonic buffalo acts as a metaphor for the "herds" of white men who have inundated Indian lands (which, ironically enough, the Lakota had in turn forcibly usurped from their enemies the Arapaho, the Shoshoni and the Cheyenne). Illustrating that enmity existed not only between red and white men, the Lakota must fight for their lives when attacked by a war party of Crow braves. Wild Bill and Crazy Horse eventually collaborate in the killing of the beast, thus uniting their spirits on the metaphysical plane.

Despite all its many shortcomings, the film stays laudably sympathetic to both the plight of the Indian and the bison. Italian FX men Carlo Rambaldi and Mario Chiari's animatronics for the snorting, galloping monster are often most impressive indeed. Supernatural undercurrents are stressed by rattlesnake-shake percussion on British composer John Barry's moody soundtrack. Equally paranormal (except in the Spaghetti Western Cosmos!) is Bronson's one-time feat of discharging fully *nine* "blue whistlers" without even reloading his trusty five-shooter.

Dialogue is often dark and unusually worded. Despite some clichéd bigoted statements ("Like Bill Sheridan said: 'I ain't never seen a good Indian that wuzn't *dead*!'"), Wild Bill essentially respects the Native Peoples, and he evolves as a person during the course of the screenplay, culminating in his becoming Sampson's spiritual blood-brother in time for the closing reel ("Truly we are brothers born from the same belly!"). Adding a grim touch are views of mountainous piles of bleached buffalo bones; the partial remains of millions of "spikes" slaughtered following the advent of the trigger-happy White Man with his overkill, take-from-the-environment-without-ever-putting-anything-back-into-it-but-crap mentality.

And speaking of white men, the ordinarily stalwart Stuart Whitman plays a dirty-mouthed drunk and the great Slim Pickens is Abel, a crusty stage driver who unexpectedly encounters the monstrous buffalo ("Whut in Hades Hell is *that*?!"). Jack Warden's cranky character ("You know damn well brave men *don't* backshoot!") is christened *Ochinee* ("one-eye") by the Indians and refers to the white buffalo as "Ol' Nicodemus" (i.e., the Devil himself)…nothing short of Armageddon itself. Kim Novak slinks up the saloon as the aptly-named "Poker" Jenny, a mature booze floozy. In the mountain town of Featherman, John Carradine plays a scungy, scroungey undertaker, who (like Klaus "Loco" Kinski in Sergio Corbucci's eloquent snowbound Spaghetti Western **THE GREAT SILENCE** [*Il grande silenzio*, 1968, Italy]) stores his corpses in the snow to keep 'em fresh. Also featured in the cast is peplum/Spaghetti Western alumnus Dan Vadis.

Lovers of Westerns and monster movies both would do well to get **THE WHITE BUFFALO** in their sights, as it's stood the test of time rather well, all things considered. And gimme that giant, charging, bellowing glorified Muppet—which at least looks like it's an actual part of the movie, rather than appearing pasted-on—over some clinical and lifeless CG critter any day!

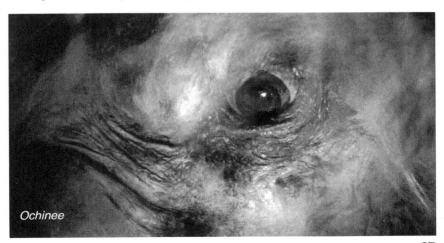

Ochinee

ANAK NG BULKAN

(*"Son of the Volcano"*)

Reviewed by Steve Fenton

Philippines, 1959. D: Emmanuel Rojas

Anglo Filipino tag-lines: *"The Science Fiction Thriller That Took One Year To Make! ...From Out Of This World Comes This Monster Bird On A Rampage Of Destruction. SEE! Downtown Manila Destroyed By A Monster Bird! SEE! Giant Ships Sank* [sic]*, Planes Swept From The Skies! SEE! Bullets, Shells, Rockets And Bombs Bounce Off This Monster Bird!"*

Unidentified soldier, speaking into walkie-talkie: *"Monster over volcano! Monster over volcano!"*

Produced by Premiere Productions, then one of the Philippines' biggest studios, the main title of

this thinly-veiled if nonetheless distinctively Pinoy **RODAN / THE GIANT CLAW** imitation is superimposed over a passable miniature of a smoking volcano, and helps establish a fitting ominous mood which is only slightly jeopardized by the somewhat inappropriate—at least to these jaded ears—theme music (composed by Tito Arevalo, later to provide scores for a great many locally-shot horror/exploitation flicks, the *Blood Island* series included; in fact, some of the very strains heard here later turned up in Gerardo de Leon's and Eddie Romero's **BRIDES OF BLOOD** [1968, Philippines]!).

Shot in moody monochrome by Ricardo Marcelino (with optical FX photography handled by the film's director Emmanuel Rojas), **ANAK NG BULKAN**—which was apparently originally released in serial form to theaters in its homeland—begins on a highly promising note as the residents of a rural village on one of the nation's more out-of-the-way islands are alarmed by the ominous and none-too-distant rumbling of the aforementioned volcano, which is on the brink of eruption and causes an earthquake prior to potentially blowing its top. Suspecting that the end is nigh, terrified townspeople congregate at the local Roman Catholic church to pray. In a bit of dramatic action which must have looked most frightening indeed to any devout Catholics in the audience, the crucifix stood atop the altar teeters precariously due to the seismic upheaval, seemingly about to topple right over; one can well imagine the expressions of horror on the faces of many audience members at the mere prospect... not that it actually *does* topple over, natch.

Unearthed by the geological disturbance, an egg (roughly the size of an ostrich's and rather resembling a watermelon) comes rolling down the mountainside like a rugger ball and lands amidst the smoldering rubble. As suddenly as it had begun, the rumbling and shaking within the earth stops. Signaling a symbolic all-clear (as well as perhaps providing a bit of tongue-in-cheek foreshadowing?) a crowing rooster is juxtaposed with the now-stilled volcano. Following this near-miss disaster, the villagers set about tidying up the wreckage left by the quake. In its aftermath, a little boy and girl—Bentoy and his baby sister Anita—discover the egg, and when Bentoy impulsively cracks it open, a live avian chick is found inside (rather than any sort of FX creation, an actual living bird of a chicken-like species is shown). Bentoy thereafter raises the bird—named Golat—as his pet, and it begins to develop into quite a formidable fighting cock. When Bentoy's abusive father figure Canuto (the *Blood Island* series' Bruno Punzalan, who is at times here rather reminiscent of Japanese character-acting great Takashi Shimura) takes a cane to him in punishment, the bird attacks the man. Rightly fearing reprisals following this attack, the boy runs away from home, taking the bird and his dog with him, whereafter they hide-out in a cave. As it matures, the creature grows less chickenishly scraggly and more majestically aquiline. When the unsuspecting sleeping Bentoy is menaced in the middle of the night by a stalking albeit rubber cobra—which is shot POV, rather like the one in **CULT OF THE COBRA** (1955, USA)—the eagle-like, hawk-eyed Golat swoops down on the serpent, thus saving its human benefactor (insert authentic mondo-style shot of bird of prey's talons mangling snake here!). When the brutal Canuto—who's such a dirtbag, he later murders the juvenile hero's mutt with a machete—attempts to ravish the heroine Julia (the luminously lovely Edna Luna), Golat once again flaps to the rescue like an airborne Rin Tin Tin with feathers. Sometime later, Golat has grown to roughly the size of a draft horse—albeit winged like Pegasus—and little Bentoy fits him with a homemade bridle and reins and rides him bareback through the sky, taking his kid sis along for the ride. Mounted on the feathered flapper's back, the two children go off on an aerial joyride, soaring high above the rooftops of the city of Manila, and this expectedly provokes a panic reaction amongst the populace down on terra firma (the English phrase "*Flying saucer!*" is heard used by more than one extra to describe the UFO!). Interestingly enough, once the main bulk of the action shifts to metropolitan Manila, more English words and phrases begin to pepper the dialogue with increasing frequency.

Our big bird bad boy Golat (a play on "Goliath") isn't in the least bit frightening to behold, but then he isn't supposed to be, being essentially a benignant creature. Looking about equal parts pigeon and vulture in its pre-adult form, it appears just vaguely sinister enough to unnerve those who view it as an ill omen, but is still cuddly-cute enough to appeal to the kids in the audience, even with its big beak and formidable talons. It's only after the previously peaceful creature turns bad and begins its one-bird war against all human civilization that Golat starts to look a lot more fearsome (much "scarier" [note quotes] than the marionette superchicken seen in **THE GIANT CLAW**, that's for sure!).

A squadron of Philippine Air Force (PAF) F86F Saber jet fighters is scrambled from Nichols Field,

and give chase. In a tense scene, due to the wind caused by the increased airspeed necessary to evade the jets, Bentoy's sis is blown off Golat's back and falls to certain doom, only to be snatched out of mid-air in the nick of time by the winged wonder's giant claw. Sick of being misunderstood and dumped on by mankind and now out for revenge, what does Golat the gliding goliath do? Why, he sinks a ship at sea—a snippet of footage pinched from **GOJIRA** (1954, Japan)—by dropping what appears to be a pile of luminescent, incendiary *bird shit* on it, that's what; thus turning it into a blazing inferno! I kid you not. I had to replay this scene several times just to make sure my eyes weren't playing tricks on me; and sure enough, unless I missed something somewhere,

Monsters and their toys, jets are no match for these beasties! top to bottom: **THE GIANT CLAW** (1957), **ANAK NG BULKAN** (1959), and **RODAN** (1956)

that's how things appear to go down, so until I hear confirmation to the contrary from a reliable source, that's how I'm choosing to interpret it (i.e., that the bird "dropped bombs" to sink the ship; an offensive—and just plain *offensive*!—tactic which it doesn't reuse elsewhere, more's the pity). Having grown to still more gigantic proportions and evidently gone completely and irredeemably over to the dark side, Golat is now feared even by his devoted rearer Bentoy, who still loves and pities him nonetheless, despite what he has become as a direct result of Man's inhumanity to Monster. The armed forces on land, at sea and in the air are mobilized against the now all-out hostile creature (conveniently allowing for the insertion of plentiful stock shots of ack-ack and other artillery attempting to shoot it down, as per standard practise in such films regardless of their national origin). In another scene, the high winds caused by the low-flying Golat send a tidal wave surging through Manila, and an elemental combination of air, water and fire reduces the city to ruins. This entire sequence is choppy and chaotically constructed, but it rather suits the context and adds a definite dynamism which allows us to overlook all the sluggish spots earlier in the narrative.

While Golat subsequently returns to roost on the side of the active volcano which spawned it (hence the title), "Operation Goliath" is launched by the military ("Boy, I hope that monster doesn't come back until we're ready!" exclaims the CO while he and his command keep watching the skies). In another wild sequence, the creature is strafed by

missile-firing jets; in what amounts to one of the coolest individual images in the movie, a model plane flies into the monster's open beak and explodes, rendered with irresistibly lo-tech panache. This leads into the even more explosively fiery finale, which is pretty damn exciting, all things considered.

It's not until quite late into the action that our main adult hero Capt. Arturo Barba (played by Fernando Poe, Jr. [1939-2004], future star of many an "Adobo" Western and other actioners) first shows up in his military uniform. Popularly known as "Da King", Poe is a revered filmic figure in the Philippines, and the easygoing likeability of his popular screen persona is much in evidence here, even if his performance is a little uneven in spots. Acting is for the most part quite naturalistic, however. Indeed there is an almost documentary-like *cinéma vérité* tone to many scenes, despite the wholly fantastical framework of the scenario and all the largely glaringly unrealistic if lovable FX work depicting the all-out fantasy elements. Much as you might expect in any comparable Hollywood film of the period, a lot of the running time comprises scenes of domestic soap opera and schmaltzy lovey-dovey. For instance, despite what a dishy dreamboat she thinks he is, gorgeous, doe-eyed heroine Luna really plays hard to get with Poe our hero... and then some! Due to the heavy Vatican influence on the culture of the predominantly Roman Catholic Philippine Islands, onscreen osculation (i.e., mouth-to-mouth kissing) was forbidden to be shown in Filipino films until the surprisingly late year of 1963, when that barrier came crashing down with a vengeance, and an escalation in movies exploiting the formerly forbidden allure of kissing occurred (later still came full-on full-frontal nudity, then later still hardcore porn). Having been made at the tail-end of the more restrictive preceding decade, in ANAK NG BULKAN, no actual kissy-face is shown. For instance, in one scene after repeatedly turning her face away from his whenever he has tried to smooch with her up till this point, when Luna at last puckers-up (albeit sight unseen) for Poe in order to receive her first kiss, the camera coyly pans down to show their feet rather than their faces as she rises up onto her slippered tiptoes in front of her much taller hunk; an action clearly meant to indicate they have just done the ol' liplock, albeit completely out of frame so as not to risk the wrath of the Church-appointed Board of Censors for Motion Pictures. Oddly enough, this enforced restraint adds a quite titillating eroticism to the scene.

Further welcome titillation is provided during chastely tasteful cheesecake scenes showing sarong'd native washerwomen (sexy Filipina maidens all) gossiping up a storm while doing their laundry together down at the local waterhole. Things get that much sexier still when all her giggling sistren collectively splash water on our secondary heroine, Mameng (Miriam Jurado, who, as it happens, went on to become one of the "most-kissed" actresses of the '60s in Pinoy cinema). We shortly segue into a charming scene—about on a par with something in a Dorothy Lamour "island girl" movie of the '40s—where Mameng sneaks off to doff her sarong and go skinnydipping beneath a picturesque jungle waterfall. Once again playing it coy, as she jettisons her sole garment, the camera pans down to her feet as it falls around her ankles, and this discreet disrobing is witnessed from the bushes by our peeping tom secondary hero, Ramon (Ronald Remy, who went on to play Dr. Lorca in de Leon's and Romero's **MAD DOCTOR OF BLOOD ISLAND** [1968, Philippines]). For still another highly suggestive shot, while the "nude" girl is off swimming some distance away, she is viewed framed through the swimming-trunked hero's bare open legs as he stands on the shore, as yet still unnoticed by her. He then proceeds to rather ungallantly filch her presently unoccupied sarong, thus leaving her without a thing to wear. Later into the action, Mameng gets offended when, as an apparent in-joke, Ramon buys her a "skimpy" bathing suit (i.e., a bikini which utilizes about the same amount of fabric as a post-Vatican II nun's habit). Far from grateful, she throws it in his face, evidently a naturist, she finds it a lot more wholesome to swim in the nude rather than being forced to wear such a "provocative" garment. (Okay, enough of all this nonsense! This is a monster movie, not a nudie-cutie, and this is *Monster!*, not *Highball...*)

Scenes of destruction are well-handled, and if they did incorporate stock disaster footage, it is quite smoothly integrated due to more than competent editing. Sure, in some scenes which integrate—or so they hoped!—full-scale action with background miniatures, the matte-lines are as thick as your arm. On the poor quality print I watched, some of the crude optical compositing FX reminded me of really primitive Chroma key, as seen on old TV shows. But it is all put together more than competently, so I'm sure an English-subbed print (fat chance!) would make things a good deal easier to take. But with untranslated Tagalog dialogue, while we can sometimes hazard a guess at what's going on generally, the specific content of the wordage is indecipherable. But even with the impenetrable language barrier, I must admit that I did find some of the nicely-acted, non-cloying kid-to-kid comedic interaction stuff really charming, and sometimes even pretty intentionally hilarious; such as when our brother and sister kid heroes are shown brattily bickering with and bitching at each other in one scene. "Featuring" Ace York (a.k.a. Ace Vergel, who died in 2007) as Bentoy our boy hero and "introducing" Elizabeth Rigor as his button-cute and sassy sis Anita, the film really plays-up the kiddie angle while thankfully not talking-down to us adults. And while we're on the topic of children here, I just wanted to mention that this movie was released theatrically in its land of origin in early September of '59: a mere two months almost to the day prior to my date of birth. That said, seeing how ancient this well-worn B&W film looks nowadays makes me feel very *old* indeed!

When all is said and done (I'm winding down now, I promise!), you can criticize all its dramatic and technical failings as much as you want, but when it gets right down to it, **ANAK NG BULKAN** is virtually impossible to dislike. You have my word on it.

NOTES: The prolific Cirio H. Santiago (owner of Premiere Productions) functioned as production manager; he would direct a by all accounts much cheezier remake of the film under the same title in 1997 (ad-line: *"The Boy, The Bird and The Volcano – A legend retold, An adventure unfolds"*). Posters showed the boy hero, now known as Pedring (played by preteen Tom Taus), sat astride a goofily smiling, muppety pterodactyl-like critter: the new Golat (IMO, an archaeopteryx might have been a better casting choice). Both Edna Luna and Miriam Jurado went on to appear in Gerardo de Leon's whimsical fantasy **ANAK NI DYESEBEL** (1964, Philippines); the former-named actress playing Dyesebel, a heroic mermaid character created by comics illustrator Mars Ravelo, of *Darna* fame. Luna had originated the character onscreen in de Leon's **DYESEBEL** (1953, Philippines).

De los creadores de los efectos especiales de ALIEN, LA HISTORIA INTERMINABLE Y CONAN.

LA GRIETA

THE RIFT
(a.k.a. **LA GRIETA**)

Reviewed by Steve Fenton

Spain, 1990. D: Juan Piquer Simón

US ad-line: *"You Can't Hold Your Breath And Scream At The Same Time"*

Released way back when on N. American VHS/Beta tape by LIVE Home Video under the apropos if less than scintillating title **ENDLESS DESCENT**, I first caught this cheapjack if entertaining marine monster entry back in the early-'90s, but for some reason never got around to reviewing it for any of the various zines I used to write for (hence, I am very belatedly rectifying that state of affairs here and now!). While it was a wannabe cash-in on the brief "submarine sci-fi" trend launched by James Cameron's mega-budgeter **THE ABYSS**, I remember enjoying it a lot (at least as much, if not more so, than I enjoyed Cameron's vastly costlier epic).

Evidently due to a design flaw, a state-of-the-art nuclear-powered submarine known as the Siren 1 is lost at sea along with its eight-man crew somewhere north of Norway at great depth in the icy waters of the Arctic Ocean. The missing vessel's original designer Wick Hayes (Jack Scalia, who from some angles when the light hits him

a certain way fleetingly rather resembles a leaner-faced David Hasselhoff, but has better hair [!]) is dispatched in the Siren 2 to hopefully get to the bottom of what happened…both figuratively and literally. Certain members of the crew of the rescue sub blame Hayes for the disaster which has befallen the Siren 1, so there is much open animosity towards him when he first comes aboard the Siren 2. While most of the other crew members are civilians, the sub is placed under the command of Capt. Phillips (R. Lee Ermey, a real-life asshole who typically played assholes onscreen, as here) and his second-in-command, Lt. Nina Crowley, a U.S. Navy research scientist (Deborah Adair, who is at times a Debra Winger dead-ringer). Some distance into their voyage, the Siren 2 picks up—what *appears* to be—an electronic signal from the Siren 1's black box emanating from a rift in the seabed at the extreme depth of 27,000 feet.

Amazingly enough, algal plant life—which, as with land-based plants, can only exist where there is sufficient sunlight available for the process of photosynthesis to occur—is discovered thriving down in the rift. "Nothing's normal at these depths", says Adair upon receiving a sample of seaweed for analysis. While exploring in the kelp forest after finding the messed-up corpse of a Siren 1 crew member, a diver is shortly attacked and gorily dispatched by a many-tentacled *something* lurking amidst the waving fronds of unnatural algae. Deeper down in the rift, the Siren 2 is thereafter engulfed by a gigantic amorphous organism resembling some sort of albino sea slug on supersteroids. Their encounter with this googly-eyed critter, whose gelatinous body mass fouls the ship's turbo intakes, drags the Siren 2 to a still greater depth. At last coming to the bottom of the seemingly bottomless rift, the sub enters a long cave tunnel, via which they gain access to (quote) "a recessed, naturally pressurized subterranean cavern". And here is where the fun really begins! Assuming, that is, you're used to having your thrills on a budget which would have barely covered the coffee and donuts tab on Cameron's movie.

When the crew dons gas masks and white plastic industrial overalls—talk about *cheap* costumes!—in order to go on an exploratory foray into the toxic environment of this deep sea grotto, they are attacked by a species of giant, burrowing marine worm whose oversized faceted eyes look like mammalian brains and whose bite causes instant paralysis…then shortly a horrible death. They also encounter something resembling a cross between an XL lamprey and a cobra, plus some more highly-evolved life-forms which appear to be hybrids of reptiles and deep sea fish (one of these chews a crew member's lower leg off in phony if gory fashion). In the depths of the labyrinthine caverns, the explorers discover a derelict scientific research laboratory which the sneaky Pentagon has done its best to keep a secret, and with good reason. From old computer data tapes found in this lab, the would-be rescuers learn that a "DNA accelerator" and "trans-genetics"—good ol' gene-splicing—have been used to unnaturally speed-up the natural process of evolution and create a variety of monstrous mutations derived from intermixing the genes of different marine organisms, apparently at random. Nearby, an as-yet unhatched brood of amniotic sacs are found containing fetal fishman-type creatures ("Damn thing looks almost human!"). Our heroes endeavor to ensure that none of these artificially created evolutionary aberrations survive ("God forbid they reach the surface!"), also trying their best to mop-up the remainder of the other less highly-evolved creatures.

Creator of the various species of creature and special makeups was Colin Arthur, who clearly only had limited resources at his disposal, but makes the best of it. For instance, a key component in the construction of some unnaturally proliferating seaweed in the sub's shipboard lab seems to have been sheets of that "poppable" bubble plastic, albeit spray-painted chlorophyll green so as to increase the realism (!). When we finally do get to see them well into the narrative, most of the (quote) "abundant mutants" are never really shown in their entirety, and their victims are typically seen simply being grabbed by a claw or tentacle lunging in from out of frame. Promising advance promotional stills which I originally saw in an issue of France's glossy *Mad Movies* prozine at the time of **THE RIFT**'s production made the monsters appear a lot more impressive than they actually are onscreen, but it's not so much their fabrication which is at fault, it's more the coy presentation of them (both the cinematographer and the editor sometimes seem to be trying their best *not* to show them; although possibly this might have been a personal directorial decision on Piquer Simón's part).

Blatant product placements include sundry views of cans of both a well-known brand of soft drink and beer. Evidently to show what a bad-ass he is, Ermey's character crushes an empty can of the latter product in his fist to emphasize a point, and is immediately pegged as a real son-of-a-bitch by those under his command (e.g., "You can play with your pecker for all I care, just so long as you don't do it in my control-room! *Dismissed!*"). The scenes where everybody reacts to imaginary underwater turbulence by throwing themselves all around the cabin while the cameraman shakes his rig violently are every bit as funny as those similar scenes with Captain Kirk and his crew aboard the U.S.S. Enterprise on *Star Trek*.

Scalia worked largely on the idiot box, including—fittingly enough considering his looks and acting chops—the never-ending daytime soap opera *All My Children*. As per cliché here, his sometimes-a-bit-of-a-dick Wick character had previously been dipping his wick in onscreen former flame Adair's aloof, by-the-book sailorette/scientist, and their relationship had ended badly. This has predictably enough left plenty bad blood between them (mostly on her side). Just as predictably, before you can say "Methinks the lady doth protest too much", the pair begin to warm to each other once again. En route to the rift of the title, we get a whole lot of stiltedly-acted "conflict" between crewmen, especially Scalia's and Ermey's antsy characters, neither of whom carry much conviction even when defiantly opposing one another at every turn. As a bespectacled, nerdy computer tech named Robbins, Ray Wise—who gives about the most convincing performance on display here (which really isn't saying too much, I'm afraid)—fills a supporting part while doing little else but stare at monitors and methodically push buttons, leaving most of the rest of the cast to push each other's.

A "startling twist" (note quotes) involving a certain aforementioned member of the Siren 2 crew comes as no surprise at all, but I'll refrain from spoiling it for you by divulging their identity. About the biggest surprise to be had here is the fact that nobody aboard the sub turns out to be a cyborg working in league with the evil controlling conglomerate!

Making a quickie cameo appearance, Edmund Purdom was cast in a throwaway part for a single scene as a Norwegian named Steensland—dapperly draped CEO of the all-powerful Contec Corp. —who is seen sitting behind still another desk (in the latter stages of his career he played a lot of characters whose asses were seemingly fused to their office chairs!).

Francisco Braña Pérez (1934-2012), better known as "Frank" Braña, is generally best known—if at all—for appearing in upwards of 50 spaghetti and paella westerns, spanning the entirety of the Euro western cycle. For Piquer Simón's **MYSTERY ON MONSTER ISLAND** (a.k.a. *Misterio en la isla de los monstruos*, 1980, Spain/USA)—allegedly based on a Jules Verne story—Braña hunted cameo'ing castaway pirate Paul Naschy with a Winchester and sixgun while in search of a fabulous fortune in gold bullion. Even if he only appeared in the prologue sequence to shortly croak at the feet of slumming Brit guest star Terence Stamp (!), that bizarre film (fitting dialogue quote: "Monster turkey! It was an enormous *turkey!*"), shot with "live" audio, provided Braña with a rare opportunity to artic-

ulate his dialogue using his own guttural Spanglish accent. The actor also appeared in Piquer Simón's second Verne filmization **WHERE TIME BEGAN** (a.k.a. *Viaje al centro de la tierra / "Journey to the Centre of the Earth"*, 1980, Spain), co-starring Jack Taylor, who encounters a number of goofy prehistoric reptiles and a giant gorilla at the Earth's core. Braña continued his if by no means lucrative then at the very least fairly dependably steady professional association with Piquer Simón on our present title. By the time he appeared in **THE RIFT**, Braña's hair had grown whiter—and his eyebrows even bigger and bushier than usual!—but he still appeared in fine physical fettle otherwise in his supporting role as Siren 2 nuclear subber Müller, whose few minor lines were dubbed with a *faux* German achzent. First seen wearing a pristine white wife-beater, his character is killed off—absorbed alive by a mobile mass of mutated seaweed—at the orders of guest star Ermey.

Severely downscaled cribs are made from such Hollywood monster movies as **ALIEN** (1979), **THE THING** (1982) and **ALIENS** (1986), etc. As with much of J.P. Simón's filmography, his attempts at generating intensely suspenseful drama have a tendency to fall flatter than a halibut (or worse yet, register as unintentionally hilarious due to under- and/or overplaying). For instance, after only narrowly escaping total destruction, one of the two female cast members (Ely Pouget) is heard to "exclaim" in a totally bored-sounding monotone, "Phew, that just saved our collective asses", her relief at having narrowly survived tangible (*not!*). Token African-American crewman John Toles-Bey casually drops at least two "white boy" jokes, but his honky crewmates

In the 90s I was thumbing through a laserdisc cut-out bin at Camelot Music and was very happy to find **ENDLESS DESCENT**. A fun film with an even better score and sound effects in stereo. I sampled large chunks of the film's soundtrack for use in an extended electronic tune I composed in 1999 called "One Ugly Baby". ~ Tim Paxton

tastefully refrain from responding to his reverse racism in like kind.

Clocking-in at about 30 seconds short of 80 minutes (end credits inclusive), you could almost watch this thing *twice* in about the same amount of time it would take you to watch **THE ABYSS** only once. Even at half the length and untold millions of dollars less the budget, for my money **THE RIFT** totals at least double the entertainment value, even if it doesn't have a single original idea in its head.

THE VAMPIRE OF THE OPERA

Reviewed by Dennis Capicik

Italy, 1961[1964]. D: Renato Polselli

Although Riccardo Freda's **THE DEVIL'S COMMANDMENT** (a.k.a. **I VAMPIRI**, 1956) is credited as Italy's first post-war horror film, it wasn't until the success of Roger Corman's numerous Poe adaptations and Hammer's horror pictures—in particular Terence Fisher's **HORROR OF DRACULA** (1958, UK)—that Italian filmmakers jumped on the horror bandwagon. Mario Bava's **BLACK SUNDAY** (*La maschera*

del demonio, 1960) was the most widely acknowledged, but Renato Polselli's **THE VAMPIRE AND THE BALLERINA** (*L'amante del vampiro*, 1959) was actually the first to try and mimic Fisher's film, although with the added bonus of dancing ballerinas, whose routines were more akin to burlesque numbers than anything seen at a prestigious dance academy. A couple years later, prolific screenwriter Piero Regnoli directed his "sexy vampire" pic with the even steamier **THE PLAYGIRLS AND THE VAMPIRE** (*L'ultima preda del vampiro*, 1961), which, for the time, pushed nudity to its limits, with Maria Giovannini parading around topless for much of the film's running time. Directed in 1961 but not actually released until 1964 as *Il mostro dell'opera* (a.k.a. *Il vampiro dell'opera*), for **THE VAMPIRE OF THE OPERA**, director Renato Polselli returned to the horror genre—which he helped kickstart in Italy—with a rather distinctive effort that plays with time, reincarnation and, yes, even invisible barriers of the supernatural kind.

As with most of these early Italian gothic cheapies, a group of dancers, led by Giulia ("Barbara Howard"/Marisa Barbaria) and their director Sandro ("Mark Marian"/Marco Mariani), come across an abandoned theatre, which is perfect for their next production. Of course, unbeknownst to them, it's also the resting place of an accursed vampire named Stefano ("John McDouglas"/Giuseppe Addobbati), whom Giulia

has also seen in some earlier premonitions. Despite the persistent warnings from the theatre's caretaker, Achille ("Albert Archett"/Alberto Archetti), the group decides to stay nonetheless, and it's soon revealed that Giulia has an uncanny resemblance to Stefano's jilted lover Laura.

As evidenced by the above synopsis, this appears to be yet another standard gothic horror thriller, but what sets this particular effort apart are Polselli's rather unique obsessions, which involve everything from light S/M scenarios (what *is* his fascination with pitchforks?!) to philosophical discussions on love, and just life in general, which are all served up in typically pulpy fashion. Many of Polselli's obsessions really came to the fore during the more permissive '70s in such films as **DELIRIUM** (*Delirio caldo*, 1972), **BLACK MAGIC RITES** (*Riti magie nere e segrete orge del trecento...*, a.k.a. **THE RE-INCARNATION OF ISABEL**, 1973) and the wonderfully *outré*-titled **REVELATIONS OF A PSYCHIATRIST ON THE WORLD OF SEXUAL PERVERSION** (*Rivelazioni di uno psichiatra sul mondo perverso del sesso*, 1973), which for the time pushed the limits of the Italian censors; but it's in this early formative effort that Polselli's "stamp" first became truly evident.

The opening is particularly interesting, as a woman (who we soon learn is Giulia) is pursued by the titular vampire through numerous castle corridors and she comes across an invisible barrier, which seems to trap her in some otherworldly dimension. Ugo Brunelli's camera is rarely still, and the tilted angles and occasional under-cranked action amp-up the weirdness even more, while Aldo Piga's traditional score is underpinned by cackling and an almost piercing use of that eerie old horror standby, the Theremin. It's certainly an attention-grabber, but Polselli still manages to keep viewer interest during many of the film's slower parts with some *fumetti*-styled homage as the men of the theatre troupe wear some rather striking skeletal costumes, while much of the female cast parades around in skimpy "baby doll" pajamas. It's also during many of the establishing scenes that Polselli gets to indulge in many of his philosophical ruminations about relationships (e.g., "Feelings never last forever, but everyone pretends they do"), while they practice a rather salacious "Charleston" as Achille the caretaker scours the catacombs with a worried look on his face. One of the film's boldest and most controversial scenes of the time is a rather startlingly overt lesbian scene, and, although nothing is shown, the dialogue is certainly on the risqué side ("Do you also believe that 'friendship' between two women is purer?"), as they seductively caress each other in one of the many darkly-lit rooms within the castle.

It isn't too long before many of the cast members begin to feel uncomfortable in this abandoned castle—as one girl points out, "The dressing rooms look like Etruscan tombs, the doors creak, the windows look like eyes...the curtains like vengeful ghosts..." Stefano finally makes an appearance and most of the girls are immediately intrigued, but one of them quickly realizes he doesn't cast a reflection in her mirror as she adjusts her makeup, and freaks out. Giulia is also magnetically drawn to him and feels as if she is "plunged into a lost dream", and it's at this point that many of Polselli's "manias" are fully realized. Stefano has a dungeon full of scantily-clad women chained to a wall as they hungrily try to bite anyone that enters his "chamber of horrors", and when Stefano brings Giulia into his hidden lair, that trusty old pitchfork makes another appearance as he wrestles her into submission under its pointy end. Meanwhile, many of the dancers become entranced under his power and begin dancing, screaming and moving furiously while trying to escape the stage they are trapped in by that unexplained invisible barrier; Algo Piga's music also explodes into a jazz-infused barrage of horns and percussion, which adds immensely to the disorientation and confusion. While the actual story isn't anything new, Polselli's offbeat approach to the material is certainly engaging and unique, and, thankfully, the entire film moves quickly through its rather brief running time (80m.), which doesn't allow one time to think too hard about some of the plot's inconsistencies.

Released in France on DVD from Artus Films under their "*Gothique Italien*" line, the transfer of this once exceedingly rare film is taken from both French and Italian prints. While the French print looks considerably sharper, numerous dialogue scenes from the first half—which were spliced in from an inferior Italian print—were either excised completely or shortened. Unfortunately, many of these extra scenes aren't too far removed from the quality seen on a blurry VHS tape, but what sets this particular DVD apart from Artus' other releases are the inclusion of English subtitles, so all is forgiven. Just the same, the quality fluctuations can be distracting to some viewers, so be aware. Extras are rather sparse, including an informative (if French-only) interview with filmmaker and film historian Alain Petit, a cool but short poster/still gallery and trailers for other titles in this series.

THE RIFT

STEVE DITKO MONSTERS! RULE —SANS RULES...

By Stephen R. Bissette

Monster! readers should know up front that I've written and sung the praises of the
*Charlton Silver Age monster comics at length—and will again—online and in print,
but here and now, it's Charlton's popular 1960s* Gorgo *comics series I'm writing
about, specifically Craig Yoe's most handsome Yoe Books/IDW reprint edition of
the complete Joe Gill (script)/Steve Ditko (art) entries in the Charlton* Gorgo *series.*

A little background: first of all, I've been in love
with Gorgo—the monster, the movie, the comic—
for over half a century, so no unbiased impartial
reading here. I've held on to every single issue
of *Gorgo* and *Gorgo's Revenge/Return of Gorgo*
(and *all* the Charlton monster comics, *Konga* and
Reptilicus/Reptisaurus primary among them) to
the present day, and won't bore you with my own
ongoing relationship with 'em all. To paraphrase
what someone once wrote as a comment when
I celebrated the publication of Tim Lucas's
biography of Mario Bava, *Mario Bava: All
the Colors of the Dark*, "you're gonna get that
book pregnant". Well, same goes for Gorgo—*all*
incarnations of Gorgo.

Now, the 2013 Yoe Books/IDW *Gorgo* reprint volume—*Ditko Monsters Vol. 1: Gorgo*, which was followed a few months later with *Ditko Monsters Vol. 2: Konga*—ignores much of the Charlton *Gorgo* series to (understandably) favor *only* those issues drawn by Steve Ditko, who one year after lavishly delineating Charlton's initial issue of *Gorgo* (adapting the MGM/King Brothers movie) would co-create one of the most famous and popular characters in comicbook history, *The Amazing Spider-Man*, for Marvel Comics. When I was a kid, I loved *Spider-Man*, too, when it was flowing from Ditko's hand—I immediately gave up the title when Ditko left—but not the way I loved *Gorgo*.

Flashback to 1961: though it was a British feature film production, **GORGO** opened at the end of March, 1961 (as if it were designed to be my personal birthday gift just two weeks after my sixth birthday!) throughout America (opening in London in October of the same year). Giant monster movies had been raging on the big screen for almost a full decade, spawned by the one-two punch of RKO's surprise blockbuster success with a 1952 reissue of **KING KONG** (1933) and Warner Bros.' even more surprising box-office score with the indie pick-up **THE BEAST FROM 20,000 FATHOMS** (1953).

This tsunami hadn't subsided by 1960; it had only picked up steam. By 1961, two competing British studios had produced **KONGA** and **GORGO**, while producer Sidney Pink completed the Danish **REPTILICUS** (finally released, after much folderol, by American-International Pictures in 1962)—and all three became Charlton-licensed titles, as Monarch movie tie-in paperbacks and as long-lasting Charlton Comics series that long-outlived the brief theatrical runs of all three monster movies.

GORGO was bankrolled by prolific producers Frank and Maurice King—who had scored big with their import of Toho's first color *daikaiju-eiga*, 空の大怪獣 ラドン / *Sora no daikaijū radon* (a.k.a. **RODAN, THE FLYING MONSTER**, 1956/57, Japan)—and they were, as I was once told by British-born producers Richard Gordon and Alex Gordon (over a marvelous Syracuse, NY CineFest dinner orchestrated by my pal G. Michael Dobbs and Alex), rather *fixated* on their mother. Eager to both tap the giant monster boom and send a love letter to mothers everywhere, the King Brothers wrangled famed production designer/director Eugène Lourié, who previously directed and co-wrote both **THE BEAST FROM 20,000 FATHOMS** and the British **BEHEMOTH THE SEA MONSTER** (a.k.a. **THE GIANT**

BEHEMOTH, 1959), to direct. Despite his misgivings over being typecast as a monster movie director (his only other directorial effort was **THE COLOSSUS OF NEW YORK**, 1958, for Paramount), Lourié made the most of the opportunity, working from a solid script credited to "John Loring" and "Daniel Hyatt" (actually blacklisted screenwriters Robert L. Richards and Daniel James). After **GORGO**, Lourié resigned himself to returning to production design and art direction, never to direct again, though **GORGO** was a hell of a monster movie in its day.

Charlton—already renowned in the industry for paying their writers and artists the lowest rates in the industry and printing their books on the cheapest pulp paper possible—really milked the license. As in the movie, maternal love was the heart and soul of the Charlton *Gorgo* mythos, and I loved *Gorgo* as I loved few other comic books. *Gorgo* ran 23 issues, plus three *Gorgo's Revenge/Return of Gorgo* issues—28 issues in all, if one counts the giant-sized *Fantastic Giants* as #24 (which Charlton did, in its indicia).

Only a handful of that run sported Steve Ditko's artwork, but oh, what a handful! They're all here, in *Ditko Monsters Vol. 1*, and to put it simply, a more lavish commemorative collection could not be imagined. And, as if perfectly timed to joint release, VCI released a brand-new **GORGO** DVD/Blu-ray restored edition about one week before the Yoe Books/IDW *Gorgo* reprint volume arrived. What could be better?

So, right from the start: my hearty congratulations to editor Craig Yoe and designer Clizia Gussoni for producing such a lovely book. It's really quite exquisite, a hefty hardcover offering 224 full-color pages, measuring 8.5 x 1.1 x 11 inches and weighing in just over three pounds. The cover is lovingly textured with a faux reptile-skin scale pattern, the interior archival paper stock is the *best possible reprint* of a series previously peppered with a scattershot cheapjack reprint history, to say the least.

Now, this material has been available, piecemeal, in other formats, but none as comprehensive or sterling as this. Consider what came before, in terms of reprint volumes (and aside from Charlton's own reprint, it's *all* a progression of pirate editions):

> 1. *Gorgo* #24/*Fantastic Giants*, Charlton Comics, September 1966; reprints the complete *Gorgo* #1 and *Konga* #1 movie adaptations, plus two new Ditko monster stories.

Cover of the first *Gorgo* comic; artist unknown, but it is not Steve Ditko.

> 2. *Attack of the Mutant Monsters*, A-Plus Comics, 1991; black-and-white one-shot reprinting *Gorgo* #1 and #3, with Gorgo's name relettered to "Kegor."

> 3. *The Ditko Reader*, Pure Imagination, 2002; *Gorgo* #4 cover is the only *Gorgo* material reprinted herein. Editor/publisher

Greg Theakston ("Earl P. Wooton") got around to reprinting some of Ditko's *Gorgo* and *Konga* material in:

4. *Steve Ditko: Angry Apes 'n' Leapin' Lizards*, Pure Imagination, 2011, a trade paperback black-and-white volume reprinting select *Gorgo* and *Konga* stories.

So, as a book, a physical entity, and the almost-ideal collected edition imaginable, Yoe's *Ditko Monsters, Vol. 1: Gorgo* is the best-collected edition to date, and likely to remain so for our lifetimes (who's going to put out a companion or competing volume?).

As for the *contents*, written by Joe Gill and drawn by Steve Ditko: well, I warned you from the outset. I love these comics stories, and they've aged beautifully for this Monster Kid. As I mentioned, I still have every issue of *Gorgo* in my collection, and I revisit them every few years. Furthermore, I have extensive emotional, associational, and experiential baggage for the true then-contemporary, now-historical context of these *Gorgo* issues; having been *just* the right age to experience almost the whole of Ditko's 1960s work *as it was published* (including his work in Wally Wood's comics prozine *Witzend*, his reach for true independence and creator-ownership), I cannot impartially revisit these stories, this artwork.

Ditko was omnipresent in the 1960s: Ditko was reveling in a succession of creative peaks, and it's no exaggeration to say in hindsight that every month seemed to offer a fresh dose of Ditko in the 1960s, via his steady stream of work in Charlton Comics, Marvel Comics, DC Comics, Tower, Warren's black-and-white horror comics magazines, and even oddball surprises (like Charlton's *Mad Monsters* #1, or Wally Wood's mail-order-only *Witzend*, which I discovered via the late, great Bhob Stewart's writeup in *Castle of Frankenstein*).

Long dismissed as inferior to his Marvel and Warren 1960s work, these Charlton monster comics were and remain quite *marvelous*, in every sense of the word.

There's absolutely no need to equivocate. *Gorgo* #1 is in fact one of Ditko's finest comics art jobs, ever, brimming with energetic and ever-inventive staging, characterization, action, and imagination. His human characters are as wonderfully realized as his monsters in this movie comic, and the build-up to Gorgo's reveal is beautifully executed. It's also, arguably, along with *Konga* #1, *his first significant lengthy and sustained narrative effort*—a full issue single narrative—after well over a decade of drawing short self-contained stories. Pre-dating his key Marvel character work (which began *afterwards*), *Gorgo* #1 is a classic stretch for Ditko, and as such one of the most significant works in his Silver Age canon. Why has this never been acknowledged before?

Unfettered from the movie's man-in-suit effects constraints, while remaining true to the movie's monster design (based in part on classical Viking dragon iconography), Ditko brought Gorgo and his mother to rich, abundant, eye-popping life. While countless praises have been published about the often-lackluster Dell movie comics adaptations (and yes, I bought, read, collected, and have kept many of those—some were indeed excellent comics), I consider Ditko's movie adaptations of both *Gorgo* and *Konga* easily as good as, and better than many of, the Dell movie comics.

In fact, I defy *anyone* to find *any* panels, pages, or sequences from *any* Dell SF, horror, fantasy, or monster comic—other than John Buscema's terrific cyclops sequence for Dell's *The 7th Voyage of Sinbad* (1958) comic adaptation—that even comes close to the vivid, literally volcanic power of Ditko's work on the *Gorgo* movie tie-in comic. [*NOTE:* I am referring, of course, to the Dell movie comics only; Dell's *Tarzan, Turok Son of Stone* (and its backup *"Young Earth"*), *Kona Monarch of Monster Isle*, etc. boasted amazing monsters and monster action sequences, and I count Jesse Marsh, Russ Manning, Sam Glanzman and Alberto Giolitti among my personal cartooning heroes!] Hey, I loved and still love Jesse Marsh, but Ditko's *Gorgo* stood in stark contrast to Marsh's matter-of-fact Pal-Ul-Don-like resurrected saurians for Dell's movie comic of *Dinosaurus*; I'm an Alex Toth devotee, too, but his lackluster monsters for *The Land Unknown* comic, or Gil Kane's thudding *The Lost World* dinosaurs for Dell, don't hold a torch to Ditko's *Gorgo* movie adaptation. Ditko's artwork still resonates today, for adult readers. Note the iconic panel of Gorgo's mother smashing the phallic lighthouse—patriarchal male power, visibly usurped/destroyed (and at crotch level)—as Gorgo's mother rises from the sea in her entrance in Ditko's brilliant visualization and staging of the sequence. This was and remains potent stuff.

What was lavished, time-wise, on the licensed "special issue" debuts of *Gorgo* and *Konga* was undoubtedly impossible to emulate on subsequent *Gorgo* issues.

Were the later issues crude? Rushed? Goofy at times? You bet. But they were and are still *great* monster comics.

Nevertheless, Ditko's energy, invention, and imagination never flagged, even if the deadlines and page rates meant he simply could not devote to later issues what he had to the movie adaptations. But that didn't and doesn't inhibit the vision, vigor, or lasting entertainment value of these comics one whit, and some of the uninitiated will find unexpected delights in this collection.

Though *Gorgo* was one of the few movie monsters without nuclear bomb or radiation-related origins, iconic Cold War fears fueled the Charlton comics series. You'll find ample evidence of that in this book.

The pages are brimming with communist villains, nuclear bombs, espionage, xenophobia,

and even extraterrestrial invasions plague Gorgo and Gorgo's mom, while almost every issue was a parable—most consistent with Gill's and Ditko's own thematic career threads, from then to today—on the injustice of exploitation and those who believe themselves to be superior intellectually preying upon the perceived "weak" (Gorgo was and is, after all, an infant or adolescent of his species).

My personal favorites of those exploitation parables either find playful self-referential narrative springboards from the comic's own movie origins—such as the Americans who decide to capture and study Gorgo after seeing **GORGO** in the movies, essentially restaging Gorgo's origin for the Cold War era of US vs. Communism polemics—or those anticipating Godzilla's soon-to-manifest role as Earth's (and, by proxy, mankind's) savior, repelling invaders. In terms of the monster genre in all media, it's important to note that Gill and Ditko pioneered this "monster as savior" conceit in the 1960s—these comics predated the *daikaiju-eiga* turnabout of Toho's fifth Gojira/Godzilla epic, 三大怪獣　地球最大の決戦 / *San daikaijū: Chikyū saidai no kessen* (a.k.a. **GHIDRAH, THE THREE-HEADED MONSTER,** December 1964; US release September 1965).

My favorite of all the Ditko "Gorgo as savior" stories remains his last *Gorgo* opus, *The Return of Gorgo Special Edition #2*, "*The Creature from Corpus III*", in which humanoid/amphibian extraterrestrial invader Koorii, intent on "convincing" Gorgo that they should team up to usurp the reign of mankind, meets his match. As a morality tale aimed at young readers that effectively dramatizes and dissects the hubris and fate of an antagonist intent on exploiting perceived "tribal" bonds for malicious goals, this is as good as anything (and better than much) the Stan Lee/Steve Ditko collaborations yielded prior to *Amazing Fantasy* #15.

For instance, note the subtle foreshadowing of Koorii's fate early in the story (page 11). The positioning of the alien's fist—as if to hold Gorgo's mother (and hence the saurian species) in his grip—is calculated, and sets up the understated finale in which Gorgo holds Koorii in his own scaly fist, only to accidentally crush the alien to death. Ditko's delineation of Gorgo releasing the now-limp Koorii to drift in the sea is one of my favorite panels in all comics: Gorgo's casual release of the alien's crushed body, simply letting go of what was, to Gorgo, a broken thing of only momentary interest. That's smart, deft, elegant, simple, direct cartooning, folks, by any standard: the gesture, the composition, the offhand (and seemingly effortless) nature of it, everything. Lovely, lovely stuff.

And reread that last dialogue balloon on the final page, the story's final line—as Gorgo and Gorgo's mom rear from the sea behind the nominal scientist hero and the ever-attentive Hilda, our hero says, "I was just thinking...I wonder if the ancient dinosaurs knew what love was? I'll have to look into that..."—Gill's scripts were often quite lovely, too. Again, why has Gill been so overlooked and underrated as a writer? For genre scholars: I ask you, was there a more insightful meditation on monster love than Gill's Charlton *Gorgo* (maternal love/devotion) and *Reptisaurus* (interspecies love/courtship/parenting) comics, prior to 1970 (i.e., Len Wein and Berni Wrightson's "*Swamp Thing*" story, Bruce Jones' debut in black-and-white horror comics 'zines)? I think not.

Cover of *Famous Monsters* #11 by artist Basil Gogos (not Gorgos).

While there's clear evidence of Ditko taking shortcuts on this particular issue—note that Gorgo's teeth, by this end point in the series, no longer merited even the additional fleeting time/ink/white-out work necessary to breaking those huge triangular dental forms into the more needle-like teeth Ditko earlier drew Gorgo and Gorgo's mother sporting—Ditko was still giving his expressive all to every page, panel, and story.

The monster action was constant, too, which is (let's face it) all that most kids expected or required of a comic like *Gorgo*. I reckon all I can still pine for, as a diehard fan of these comics, are complete reprint volumes, but that's unlikely to happen. Let's face it: in 2013, Steve Ditko, not the monsters, is the "marketable star" of these comics, as Yoe's title makes clear.

Unlike other Ditko fans who have discussed their attachment to his work, I did *not* find the non-Ditko issues of *Gorgo* or *Konga* instant disappointments; unlike *Spider-Man*, which I ditched as soon as Ditko was gone, even as a kid, I stuck with *Gorgo* and *Konga* through thick and non-Ditko thin (though that, too, was in the eye of the beholder: I liked and still quite enjoy the art by the team of Bill Montes and Ernie Bache, among others). I was equally enjoying Joe Gill's scripts and the completely bizarre flavor of the Charlton monster comics as a whole, and I snapped 'em all up as I lucked into them (and caught up on missing issues early in the 1970s,

when Charlton's like these were still easily found in cheapie bins and incredibly affordable).

But, back to Ditko's work—as this collection demonstrates, he gave his all to every single outing, and even those that (in hindsight) my now-practiced pro cartoonist eye can identify as "rushed" really sing.

Craig Yoe's assessment of Ditko's work herein doesn't always jive with my own. Craig tags *Gorgo* #11 as having arguably been ghosted in part by Ditko's studio partner, Eric Stanton; I don't buy that, but who knows (only Ditko, and he isn't talking about such matters). Yoe's introduction is otherwise pretty solid, covering the wellspring movie in some detail and offering a showcase to the gorgo-eous Basil Gogos *Famous Monsters of Filmland* #11 cover art (April 1961), which is indelibly burned into the memories of all 1960s Monster Kids. We also get plenty of fun promotional art and pressbook materials from Metro-Goldwyn-Mayer's US release of the film (art by Reynold Brown, who was unhappy that MGM's publicity department went with his rough for the final poster art, rushing it into production before Brown had a chance to deliver what he considered a proper finished product), and more.

For the most part, Craig and Clizia's design work is impeccable throughout, including their ingenious play with the UPC code on the back cover (turning it into a building Gorgo is smashing). Very sharp and funny!

To my eye, the only real design lapse is in the opening spread of Craig's introduction, in which the conceptual conceit—the columns of typeset as "skyscrapers"—just doesn't read to my eye, and makes for the only design fumble in the entire volume. Nice idea, but unlike their UPC code antics, it doesn't gel; the black square paragraph breaks are a maladroit touch (thankfully abandoned after these two pages), the lack of any breathing space around the text columns where they cut into the Ditko art lifts cramp the reading and design uncomfortably. Ah, well, too bad. The rest of the intro pages, though, pleasingly balance text and ample illustration eye-candy with aplomb.

In other ways, Yoe's text leaves some key history untouched, or simply pictured without further information or context (i.e., the infamous Carson Bingham paperback from Charlton's paperback imprint Monarch, which is now back in print via Bear Manor Books). Yoe's intro research nevertheless holds true, but I have to note one major *faux pas* in the book—that *Return of Gorgo Special Edition* #2 cover *isn't* a Ditko creation. It was most definitely the work of Dick Giordano, who told me so himself back in 1977 (when I asked him after class at the Joe Kubert

School of Cartoon and Graphic Art, Inc., where Dick taught us inking). I understand the reason for Craig's error—after all, most online sources credit Steve Ditko—but one look at the art itself, particularly its Gorgo (and particularly the head and those teeth), and it's obvious Ditko had nothing to do with it.

Now, on to the downside of this book:

Damn.

Another pricey, lovely, big ol' hardcover reprint of a great cartoonist's work—*and not a fucking penny to the cartoonist.*

I hate to harp on this, but, shit. Shit howdy.

Reeeeally, IDW? *Really*, Craig?

C'mon, you're multiple volumes into Ditkoland.

Do something to address, preferably redress, this.

As a consumer, I did what I habitually do these days when I spend *anything* on *any* Ditko book or collection: I immediately sent an order off to Robin Snyder to purchase/support one or more of the Steve Ditko projects Robin and Steve have packaged and published most recently. I popped $75 off to Robin and Steve last week;

Charlton also published a comic series based on the Danish giant monster film **REPTILICUS**!

via a separate mailing, I also re-upped my subscription to Robin's ongoing newsletter *The Comics*, which has recently offered reprints of earlier (long out-of-print) *Comics* essays by Ditko, and the a whole new essay series by Ditko in the *Ditko Four-Pager* series. A lot has been said over the past couple of few years online about what Steve Ditko would or wouldn't want to have said, or say, or be said on his behalf, or be done, or whatever. Ditko continues to speak out himself, and he clearly has ongoing concerns and should be heard. Here, how about tuning in to just *one* of those?

Come on, "comics fans," discuss that. Discuss what Ditko *is writing himself*.

In short, if you're a Ditko reader, and you're *not* subscribing to *The Comics*, what are you waiting for? A one-year subscription (hell, a *two-year* subscription!) is less than the retail price of any one Yoe Books/IDW Ditko collection. Write to Robin Snyder, 3745 Canterbury Lane #81, Bellingham, WA09225-1186, or go to Bob Heer's online listing of all available Snyder/Ditko publications/comics at *http://ditko.blogspot.ca/p/ditko-book-in-print.html*, then place your mail order with Robin.

Support Ditko directly via your purchases, if that's vital to you.

And if it isn't vital to you, then *put up or shut up*, I say.

Back to *Gorgo*:

To paraphrase William Shakespeare's *Julius Caesar*, Act 3, Scene 2, some may argue that *"I come to bury Gorgo, not to praise him."* Well, perhaps—but I know I can't possibly "bury" this flourishing cottage comics reprint industry, nor does the scholar in me aching for greater access to works long entombed in pricey collectibles want to cut off the access in such books provide. But—

You know, I was *invited* to write something for the *Gorgo* collected edition, *and* the second volume collecting Ditko's *Konga* comics. Something like what you just read, only more-so—something like what I originally posted on my blog *Myrant* to be read, *for free*, and revised and expanded for this issue of *Monster!*, also for free.

I declined.

I couldn't, in good conscience, participate in either venture—much as I love Ditko's work,

much as I love and adore these two bodies of Ditko work in particular, much as I wish I *could have* contributed to them.

My decision is my own.

It wasn't and isn't a judgment of Craig Yoe, or his ongoing reprint volumes—though he is well aware of my own ethical and moral qualms with all this, and respectfully acknowledged that in reaching out to me.

The fact is, much as I enjoy the *Gorgo* reprint volume, it's everything I dreamed of—and, sadly, *everything I feared it would be*:

Ditko's name (boxoffice!) writ large, Joe Gill's name visible but modest on the front cover, but on the spine and title page, *no mention* of writer Joe Gill (the spine reads: *"Edited by Craig Yoe"*).

Oh, well, yes: Joe Gill is given his due. His name is there, small, on the front cover, and *inside*, in the context of Craig's introduction. There's even a photo of Joe, but damn it, *Joe Gill wrote this book*. It is comprised almost entirely of Joe Gill's scripts, illustrated by top-lined-in-the-title Steve Ditko.

Shouldn't they be listed on the spine as the primary authors, beyond the *Ditko Monsters* title banner?

Ironic, to say the least, in a collection of stories focusing on the exploitation of monsters unable to speak for themselves, eh? *Gorgo* passages involving blatant exploitation of the monsters take on fresh meaning in the real-world context of how these expensive reprint editions shamelessly exploit and depend upon non-payment of their creators.:

Over the past few years I've proposed (in focused *Myrant* blog posts and in various Facebook and private conversations) *multiple* creative solutions to the problems these books present.

I could have argued them all over again, campaigned for them, when I was asked to participate, but frankly, it was easier to just say "no", with my ethical reasons for declining clearly stated.

But for the record:

> * Is there *any* mention of the ongoing new published work by Steve Ditko, via publisher Robin Snyder? No, not a whisper—and certainly no full-page complimentary ad for those works.

> * Does the copyright indicia reflect, in any way, the copyright status of these works?

The Gripping Story Of A City Threatened With Annihilation By A Raging Prehistoric Monster

MM603

GORGO

Carson Bingham

This classic thriller is now on the screen as a spectacular King Brothers' Technicolor Production

British novel tie-in of the film.

Well, no. Just the book package in hand, eliminating any messy acknowledgements (that said, Craig does provide a pretty thorough overview of *Gorgo* and the comics' history in his illustrated introduction).

* And what about the primary ownership of the movie property Charlton had originally licensed in 1961? Whither *Gorgo*? One can only presume the chain-of-ownership on the original film properties and licenses for Charlton monster comics *Gorgo* and *Konga* are either too tangled, or too insignificant to the parent studios or the current corporate heirs/owners of the original feature films, to bother with these reprints. *Gorgo*, the movie, fell into public domain at some point before 1980 (it was a VHS marketplace staple, in multiple unlicensed editions), but what's its status today? Those earlier reprints I noted above—the one-shots *Attack of the Mutant Monsters, Steve Ditko: Angry Apes 'n' Leapin' Lizards*—skirted any potential licensing issues by simply avoiding use of the movie-monster names in their titles.

* Is there *anything* in these pages that would steer any *Ditko Monsters Vol. 1: Gorgo* reader to *any* means of purchasing *anything* that would benefit Steve Ditko? *No.*

So, I declined, and I'm glad, book in hand, I declined. I'll guiltily buy these books, and balance that karma by sending my money to Robin and Steve every year to support their ongoing and new ventures, and by speaking out publicly about this ongoing injustice, but there it is.

* *Ditko Monsters Vol. 2: Konga* addressed as many ethical and copyright issues as it raised further, as Ditko and Robin Snyder had already collected some of the *Konga* material in *The Lonely One* (1989). See, Ditko and Snyder reportedly *purchased the copyrights* to that material (or some of it) in the wake of Charlton closing up shop, and *The Lonely One* was reprinted directly from file *Konga* photostats from the Charlton flat files. I bow to Robin Snyder's and Ditko scholar/collector Bob Heer's accounts of that transaction, and that of other Charlton experts, on what was or wasn't purchased in that transaction, but *The Lonely One* is

still in print and available from Robin at the address listed above.

The Lonely One is a black-and-white reprint volume, which means it sports the best-possible incarnation of the material sans color; for some, though, that may not be the attraction it is for me, as a fellow cartoonist.

Others say/write: Why support inexpensive, relatively modest productions like *The Lonely One*? Surely the Yoe Books/IDW full-color reprint edition is more lavish, definitive, durable, lasting!

Sure. And as I say: *you bet your ass the printers are paid* for that lavish, full-color, hardcover edition. *Not a penny to the creators.*

   * Are there creative solutions to these ethical dilemmas?

This proliferation of high-ticket collections continues, sans even an attempt to budget for the creators whose names and work sell the books themselves. This is completely out of hand as of 2014.

As we continue to see this cottage industry of reprint volumes proliferate, it's clear we need a comics industry ASCAP (American Society of Composers, Authors & Publishers) or the like. *Something* needs to go to the creators and/or their heirs/estates for these packages.

It's not a matter, either, of whether individual creators (in this case, still-living Steve Ditko) want or will accept income. It's a matter of a creative community being fleeced regularly, their work filling pages of high-ticket books that pay little or nothing to the creators still alive or the heirs of those passed.

You bet your ass the *production* and *printing* is paid for! Look at the list of *credits* on these books: those folks have been paid, in some form or another.

That said, I have no illusions about ASCAP/BMI or such organizations. I know about the reports of corruption, unfair play, etc. But something, *something* must be initiated, and hopefully instituted; clearly, the publishers are not going to initiate anything meaningful, and surely will fight any attempt at redress (please, prove me wrong; *I would love to be wrong*). Cartoonists and comics creators in the comicbook industry (and, now, graphic novel industry) have forever resisted unionizing, as many (like myself) found ill fits and no welcomes from the Graphic Artists Guild back in the day.

Times have changed; time to change the times.

After all, if Gorgo could, we can…

———————

This is revised and expanded from a March 25, 2013 *Myrant* essay archived at: *http://srbissette. com/?p=17128#sthash.U75l0JJl.dpuf*

BOTTOM OF THE BARREL BIGFOOT

by Douglas Waltz

When I decided to take a stab at covering Sasquatch (a.k.a. Bigfoot) movies, I had no idea what I was in for. The costumes rank from really good to glorified gorilla costumes possibly bought at Wal-Mart. The budgets vary as well, so I decided to stay in the basement—the micro-budget realm of the Bigfoot, so to speak. You would think that with those parameters I would be looking at some pretty thin pickings. You would be wrong. Horribly wrong.

So, I thought it best to just start with a random sampling and, editors willing, we will revisit this subject more than once. And, before we begin, who would have thought that Bigfoot porn would ever be a thing...?!

BIGFOOT AT HOLLER CREEK CANYON

USA, 2006. D: John Poague

Bigfoot movies tend to fall on either the good or bad line. The creature is either just trying to be himself, or he's a murderous dick. In this no-budget classic in the making, it's definitely a murderous dick we are dealing with.

It's the stereotypical tale of a group of friends off to stay in an isolated cabin in the woods, unaware of what waits for them there. The main girl of the tale owns the cabin, and when they stop at a party store for supplies she is greeted by the proprietor, Ranger Rik. Since Rik is played by the one and only Ron Jeremy, at least we get what passes for acting for a few minutes.

The kids make their way to the cabin and it isn't long before we start losing them one at a time... until we arrive at a final battle between our heroine and the rampaging monster that has torn all her friends limb from limb. Even Ranger Rik is unable to escape the wrath of this bloodthirsty beast.

Here's the problem with **BIGFOOT AT HOLLER CREEK CANYON**: you don't give a *damn* about any of these characters. The guys are testosterone stereotypes who just drink and smoke weed and treat women like dirt. The girls are either busy mooning over the A/V nerd that came along for the ride or oblivious to the fact that their boyfriend will stick it to anything with a pulse. The video quality is terrible. The scripting and camera work is abysmal, and all of their money probably went to pay Ron Jeremy, who did a very good job with the character of Ranger Rik.

45

BIGFOOT'S WILD WEEKEND

USA, 2012. D: Jeff Murray

And then we go to the other end of the spectrum. Good-looking Bigfoot suit. This 'squatch is just interested in hoisting beer from fishermen's coolers and partying with as many topless girls as he can get ahold of. And since there is a group of girls from a local detention center on a camping spree, you know that toplessness and lesbianism are gonna run rampant.

Throw in a reporter from a *Weekly World News*-type rag out to cover the story for his boss and a competing television reporter showing she can make it in a man's world, and you have sex, drinking, strippers, rednecks, a bizarre revenge subplot and a ton of tongue-in-cheek (sometimes quite literally) dialogue. It reminds me of the day when Alternative Cinema would release their steady stream of softcore classic versions of whatever was big at the box office at the time... and all of them starred Misty Mundae (a.k.a. Erin Brown).

Come for the really well-done Bigfoot suit... stay for all the lovely ladies in various stages of undress.

Ronald Dean Blackwell as Chester Scroogins and Tyler Smith as his son, Billy Bo Bob steal every scene they are in. If ever there was going to be a new comedic team in film, these two should consider it. The makers of this movie should probably just put them in the next movie, because I laughed every time they were on the screen.

SHRIEK OF THE SASQUATCH!

USA, 2011. D: Steve Sessions

After that lighthearted romp we delve back into the darkness of the evil, murderous Bigfoot... but this time there's a twist.

Julie (Scarlet Salem) and Nick (Donny Versiga) are on a road trip that becomes a collision course with the titular beast.

Less of a movie and more a series of kill sequences that are unrelated to one another, eventually our two heroes arrive in the town where they have a distinct Bigfoot problem. But, there are things that make this one of the more interesting of the bunch. There is a running discussion of how come you never find the corpse of a Bigfoot. They even use the theory that Bigfoot is able to flow between dimensions.

I actually think their answer is pretty innovative, and one I haven't heard before. What is it? Yeah, I'm not giving it up that easy. Besides, this is a pretty well-done movie, and worth seeing. When I saw the director was Steve Sessions I knew I was in good hands. His underrated **DEAD CLOWNS** (2004) is one of the creepiest things I remember watching, and he generates some chilling scenes in this film as well.

The film delivers in the nudity department, as well, as it seems everyone in this town is humping like bunnies... and Bigfoot is on a coitus interruptus rampage. Maybe it's the smell? Who knows?

In a scene where Bigfoot turns over a van in which a couple are going at it, the use of a toy model of a van was pretty risky, but Sessions pulls it off. The soundtrack is great, the camerawork took me back to the '70s, and the film-look process on the video was well-done and made it feel like you were back in 1979. I applaud anyone who tries to make a period piece on a micro-budget and accomplishes what they set out to do. **SHRIEK OF THE SASQUATCH!** is definitely a step in the right direction for the Bigfoot mythos.

It's a shame the costume is just so bad. With a fixed face with no movement, it looks terrible no matter how they shoot it. Luckily, it has little screen time, but we want our Bigfoot when we watch these, don't we, guys?

SUBURBAN SASQUATCH
USA, 2004. D: Dave Wascavage

And this time around we end with what is probably the lowest of the budgets, with one of those aforementioned Wal-Mart costumes. But it might be the best of the bunch.

In the Atlantic Northeast there is an island that has become a victim of suburban sprawl. But, it has bigger problems than most. This overgrowth

of humanity has angered a local creature that usually makes its home in the Pacific Northwest.

Its name is Sasquatch, and it won't rest until it has destroyed every human it sees. Talla (Sue Lynn Sanchez), from a local Indian tribe, has been given the task of dispatching this creature. Local newspaper reporter, Rick (Bill Ushler) knows what is going on and realizes that it will be the biggest story of his life. *If* he survives.

SUBURBAN SASQUATCH is another film that questions why we never catch a Bigfoot. This one happens to be very intelligent and can actually slip between dimensions. Only someone trained to hunt the beast, like Talla, can do it any damage with special, magical arrows.

This does not stop the locals who go on a massive hunt for the beast and get their asses handed to them in the process. In the end it has to be Talla, and Rick realizes that there are things more important than a story, and he might be the only one who can make sure that Talla can complete her sacred mission.

SUBURBAN SASQUATCH is the lowest of these four films when it comes to budget, costumes and acting. But the story manages to ignore all of that and remains compelling to watch. The whole dimension-hopping aspect of Bigfoot

SUBURBAN
SASQUATCH

is rarely mentioned, but here are two films, seven years apart, that do exactly that. Also, by tying the very existence of the creature to a local Indian tribe gives more of a realistic approach to an unrealistic subject.

Sue Lynn Sanchez as Talla is a gorgeous sight to behold, and manages to keep her clothes on throughout the film. Everyone else tries and gives their best, but it is what it is: bad acting. Some of the effects made me laugh. The blood spurting is bad CGI and the scene where Bigfoot picks up a police cruiser looks like they used some computer program to cut out the picture of the car and then have it thrown through the air. Sure, we can see the actor's wrists when the gorilla—uh, I mean "Bigfoot"—sleeves ride up on the costume. Yes, it's obvious when the creature moves its mouth in close-up that someone has stuck their hand in the mask like a puppet. But, it *doesn't matter*.

The script stays smart and interesting regardless of who is delivering it, and it reminds me of an old skool shot-on-video movie from back in the days of the mom and pop video stores. Without any special film effects, it generates more of a sense of nostalgia than **SHRIEK OF THE SASQUATCH!** could ever hope for.

There you go: four Sasquatch films you've probably never heard of presented for your approval, or disapproval if they sound like a steaming pile of cryptozoological you-know-what. Next time I will show you what happens when the legendary Polonia Brothers tackle the subject.

MORE
BIGFOOT
THRILLS NEXT ISSUE!
Hairy Hominid art by
Denis St. John

48

CREATURE FEATURE

Monthly MONSTER! Column by Louis Paul

Eroticism and horror: the two perversely fit hand in hand, especially in European horror films of the late 'Fifties, and early 'Sixties. When the counterculture revolution made waves, and life as we knew it beforehand changed, suddenly the cinema was no longer the same. In the UK, stalwart British horror film studio Hammer Films got into the act by making films that featured the bared bosoms of its top-heavy leading ladies. In France, Jean Rollin, an experimental filmmaker, was pushing the envelope of softcore films with his dreamlike hallucinatory horror films featuring little dialog and plenty of lithe, thin succubae. In Spain, Jess Franco was smashing down the invisible walls of the cinematic barrier by going full-tilt and exploring any number of visualizations of the sex and horror motif.

It wasn't until the late 'Eighties that Hong Kong filmmakers began making their own unusual form of cinematic naughtiness thanks to the Category III film rating. Films rated Category III either featured a lot of nudity or tons of it... the movies careening full-tilt beyond softcore in some instances, with hardcore footage escaping the wrath of a censor's shears. After a promising start in Category III films, some actresses had nowhere to go...but straight to the bottom, appearing in all-out hardcore pornography, and sometimes ended up as the featured news item in the latest issue of a scandal-ridden tabloid.

While some Category III actresses managed to exploit their assets into crossover films before retiring into private life (think of the phenomenally-shaped Amy Yip, for example), others did not fare as well.

Pauline Chan is one example of such. Pauline Chan (or Pinyin Chen Baolian, or Bo-Lin Chan, depending on what translation of her native Shanghai name you might read) was born in China in 1973, and began modeling at age 12. While not displaying as full a bosom as rival sex starlets Amy Yip, Loletta Lee, or Pauline Wong, Pauline Chan was not thin, and her full bosom and slight lantern-jaw gave her a unique appearance in Hong Kong cinema. By the age of 18 she was appearing in a number of Category III films like **ESCAPE FROM BROTHEL** (*Hua jie kuang ben*, 1992); **DEVIL OF RAPE** (*Jian mo*, 1992); **WHORES FROM THE NORTH** (*Bei mei*, 1993), and **EROTIC GHOST STORY 3** (1993). From what can I ascertain from newsgroups on the Internet, the roles dried up for her and she began doing harder sex films in

EROTIC GHOST STORY 3

the underground. She hooked-up with an aged (over thirty years older) celebrity tycoon, and made some attempt in the late 'Nineties to revive her acting career, but then madness set in. While trying to gain entry to a dance club, she was barred. Losing her cool, she undressed and became violent. Other entries state that she tried to commit suicide (unsuccessfully) on a live television program, and became irrational in drug-fueled fits of violence. She was arrested in England in 1999 for beating someone, and briefly imprisoned. She eventually committed suicide in Shanghai, China in 2002, jumping out of a 24th-story window. When interviewed following her death, her ex-lover claimed that the bizarre behavior was due to her uncontrolled lust for sex, drug abuse...and *sorcery!* In any case, a death-

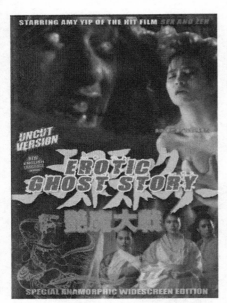

scene photo of Pauline Chan is out there…on the Internet…in repose, post-fall…with her hands tied. Yes, her hands are clearly tied. Another unsolved mystery featuring a Hong Kong sex siren, but we can still enjoy her roles, and there are a number of them…including the first film up for discussion, **EROTIC GHOST STORY 3**.

EROTIC GHOST STORY

(*Liao Zhai San Ji Zhi Zhi Deng Cao He Sheng / Liu Jai Saam Chap Chi Dang Cho Whig Seung*)
Hong Kong, 1993. D: Kai-Ming Lai
Action direction: Phillip Woko Chun Fung (Kuo Choi); Screenplay: Ginichi Rikuden, Kap Yuen-Yat; Producer: Chow Chan-tung
Cast: Pauline Chan Po-lin, Chik King-man, Shing Fui-on, Cheung King-fa, Ching-Wah Cheung

During a violent thunderstorm, a young couple takes refuge in the remains of a temple near an abandoned well in a forest. There, they encounter a Buddhist Monk (Shing Fui-on) who is a bit of a crazy wizard, as well. The Monk tells the couple that they must be careful, for the temple is haunted and they may be transported to a place of unearthly carnal desires…and it may be difficult for them to return. When the female half of the couple disappears, all hell breaks loose.

One of the stranger sights in this film is the visage of Shing-Fui-on with an uncharacteristically bald pate. Much of the cast is physically attractive, and works well within the confines of the story, which changes dramatically from the first two instalments of the *Erotic Ghost Story* series. This time there are more monsters to deal with as well as some graphic scenes that feature cannibalism. In a rare turn in a heroic role, Shing Fui-on tries vainly to gather the couple from the dimensions into which they have fallen, and return them to the place whence they started. For fans of erotica, there's plenty of gratuitous nudity and soft-core couplings.

EROTIC GHOST STORY - PERFECT MATCH

(*Liu Jai Yim Tam Ji Yau Kau*)
Hong Kong, 1997. D: Lin Yi-hung
Cast: Tsui Kam-kong, Diana Pang Dan, Teresa Mak Ka-kei, Wong Yat-fei, Keung Ka-ling

Three sexy ghosts, Ying Ying, Siu Mui and Miu Miu, were originally rabbits who were kept by the "Heaven Palace Queen Mother" (and yes, that's what the translated-into-English credits call this character!). Because these wayward animals did not want to be caged they snuck out from the netherworld and onto the Earth, where the three rabbits turned into voluptuous humans females. The fabulously well-endowed Siu Mui (actress Pang) is threatened, but she is rescued by a scholar and is thinking of returning the favor in a series of sexual ways, but the scholar's mother is suspicious of Siu Mui's background. Ying Ying and Miu Miu are also enjoying their human forms and began a series of relationships, when some jealousies arise. Of course, this being a Category III film, a number of scintillating softcore sex scenes result. But, the hot rabbit-girls' time on Earth may be short for "…Queen Mother" has already sent the being known as "Sky God" to investigate their whereabouts.

With a series of comedic situations and scenes of bickering amongst themselves, this later entry in the *Erotic Ghost Story* series is by far the worst. Although the lead featured actresses are competent—and, when in the nude, scrumptious examples of Asian beauties—the film sputters along with a series of confrontations, weakly-scripted dialog scenes, and a series of less-than-inspired sexual couplings. Made to capitalize on a film series that last saw an entry five years previous, I believe this is the last-known *EGS* film.

ROMANCE OF THE VAMPIRES

(*Xi Wo Yi Ge Wen*; *Kap Ngoh Yat Goh Man* / "Inhale My One Kiss")
Hong Kong, 1994. D: Ricky Lau Koon-wai
Action direction: Cho Wing, Yuk Su
Cast: Yvonne Yung-hung, Mondi Yau Tuet-ching, Ben Lam Kwok-bun, Louise Yuen Siu-cheung, Billy Chow Bei-lei, Yuen King-tan, Usang Yeong-fang

As in many Hong Kong horror films, two stories begin separately, then converge together before an unusual climax. In the first plot line, an attractive blind woman named Rainbow (Yvonne Yung-hung) is employed as a prostitute for an escort company where her mother works as a phone-sex operator. She does this because the money she earns will enable her to save up for an eye operation. In the second plot, a husband and wife couple shares a unique secret—they are vampires! The woman brings home men to satiate her own carnal desires, and then shares the bloodied corpses with her husband (who lies in a glass coffin).

Where the two stories become one is when the husband becomes dissatisfied with making love to his wife again and again in his glass coffin, and visits a call-girl only to discover that the blind prostitute is the reincarnation of a powerful true love from his past.

Director Ricky Lau is more commonly known for his roles as an actor in comedic vampire spoofs of the 'Eighties, most notably several entries in the popular *Mr. Vampire* series. In **ROMANCE OF THE VAMPIRES**, he combines the most controversial elements of blood and nudity that the Category III rating system will allow, along with a certain amount of drama and pathos involving a doomed love triangle. Yvonne Yung-hung was one of HK's newer starlets-in-training who appeared in a number of alarming and shocking Category III films in minor roles (**A CHINESE TORTURE CHAMBER STORY** [*Mun ching sap daai huk ying*, 1994] is the most notorious one). **ROMANCE OF THE VAMPIRES** gave her a better-than-usual chance to showcase any acting abilities she might have had, but she was seen only in a number of violent, downbeat titles. She retired from acting in '03, but recently resurfaced in recurring roles in a number of television series.

ROMANCE OF THE VAMPIRES

VISIT TO HELL

(*Sha Ru Di Yu*; a.k.a. **VISA TO HELL**, a.k.a. **SLAUGHTER INTO HELL**)
Hong Kong, 1991. D: Dick Wei
Cast: Chin Siu-ho, Kara Hui Ying-hung, Dick Wei

Two policemen who are close friends enter into a furious battle with Triad gangsters at their headquarters. One of the policemen is killed in the resulting fury, leaving his partner to ponder life without him. But, in a clever twist, both the late hero cop and the main Triad gang boss (who also dies in the gun battle) are transported to another dimension. When the cop on Earth learns of the continuing battles being fought in Hell for Right and Wrong, he enlists his other fellow (live) policeman and a Buddhist monk. In time, a small army of lawmen, aided by the monk, journey to hell to assist their buddy.

Another example of pure cinematic weirdness that can only have come from the Hong Kong! Formidable familiar martial arts villain Dick Wei was in the director's chair for this adventure, and apparently it's the only thing he ever directed. It's a shame that he did not direct more feature films, as the fight scenes are brutal and fast, with an equal amount of flying fists and bullets. The sequences set in Hell are colorful, imaginative, and clever…and ever-so-slightly tilted to the bizarre, with set direction that recalls the films of pioneering Brazilian madman José Mojica Marins.

MR. VAMPIRE

(*Geung Si Sin Sang*, "*Mr. Stiff Corpse*")
Hong Kong, 1985. D: Ricky Lau Koon-wai
S: Wong Ying, Barry Wong Ping-yiu, Si To
Cheuk Hon; P: Leonard K.C. Ho, Sammo
Hung Kam-bo
*Cast: Lam Ching-ying, Chin Siu-ho, Moon Lee
Choi-fung, Ricky Hui Koon-ying, Pauline Wong
Siu-fung, Billy Lau Nam-kwong, Yuen Wah, Wu Ma*

During the early days of the Chinese republic,
the father (Yuen Wah) of a nobleman fears that
he will return from the dead as a vampire. A Taoist priest named "Uncle Nine" or "Kao" (Lam
Ching-ying), who is known to specialize in such
cases, is brought in as a consultant to help keep
the would-be family bloodsucker at bay. Unfortunately for all involved, the heroic Van Helsing
of the Far East brings along his bumbling disci-
ples (Ricky Lau and Chin Siu-ho), both of whom
also fall in love with the ghostly-but-sexy Pauline Wong.

The first film in the influential *Mr. Vampire* series
is an entertaining glimpse at Eastern supersti-
tions and mythology. The placement of religious
incantations written on rice paper on the forehead
of the undead to keep them at bay, the holding
of one's breath lest the vampire smell you and
know your presence...are just two of the many
new forms of vampire mythology introduced to
Western culture with this film. *Mr. Vampire* also
features a cast full of Chinese actors who would
go on to make better and more commercial
films, if not one as ready-made for the cult film
market as this. Lam Ching-ying, also called the
"One-Eyebrowed Priest" due to the make-up that

he wears that makes it appear as if he has one
continuing eyebrow, would become a one-man
cottage industry in Hong Kong during much of
the mid/late 'Eighties. He starred in a number of
sequels to the original *Mr. Vampire* for the same
producers, and appeared in a similar role in other
productions for rival companies over the years.

MR. VAMPIRE 2

(*Geung Si Sin Sang Juk Jaap*, "*Mr. Stiff Corpse Sequel*")
Hong Kong, 1986. D: Ricky Lau Koon-wai
P: Sammo Hung Kam-bo
*Cast: Lam Ching-ying, Yuen Biao, Pauline Wong
Siu-fung, Moon Lee Choi-fung, Wu Ma, Sibelle
Hu (Wu Wai-jung), Stanley Fung Shui-fan,
James Tien Chun*

Taoist priest Lam Ching-ying returns for this
sequel, which also introduces the idea of
spooky-but-irritating vampire children. The *Jiangshi* (a.k.a. *Gionshi*), the hopping vampires
of Eastern mythology, are here to stay as Lam
Ching-ying and Yuen Biao battle with the sexy
Moon Lee as the Queen of the vampires. In this
first sequel, an archeologist has carelessly released a horde of vampires onto the streets of
modern day Hong Kong.

The series seemed to be heading head-first into
goofy territory with this first sequel in the popular series. Yuen Biao is added to the mix as Lam
Ching-ying's loyal-but-bumbling assistant, who
just so happens to be an expert martial artist. Set
in contemporary Hong Kong, the film makes
much use of comedic elements, such as the sequence involving a child vampire who is adopted
by a group of school children.

MR. VAMPIRE 3

(*Ling Huan Xian Sheng*, "*Mr. Unreal Goblin*")
Hong Kong, 1987. Director: Ricky Lau
Koon-wai
P: Sammo Hung Kam-bo
*Cast: Lam Ching-ying, Billy Lau Nam-kwong, Rich-
ard Ng Yiu-hon, Ho Kin Wai, Sammo Hung Kam-bo*

Lam Ching-ying and Billy Lau reunite for the
third film in the series as the vampire-fighting
Taoist priest and his assistants come across a
more deviant version of bloodsuckers, this time
around in the form of a wicked vampire-witch.
Priest Mao Ming (Richard Ng) meets Master
Gau (Ching-ying), and they join forces to combat

MR. VAMPIRE

a sexy sorceress who seeks to destroy the Earth.

Highlights in this entry include a ghostly beauty (Pauline Wang Yu-huan) who vomits bugs and maggots, another spectral beauty who flies about laughing maniacally and causing havoc. Producer Sammo Hung makes a cameo appearance as a goofy waiter, along with those annoying little hopping ghostly vampire children that one has to piss on to exterminate them. Oh, if you don't know that urinating on Chinese vampires may save your life…well…you know now!

MR. VAMPIRE 4

(*Jiang Shi Shu Shu / Geung Si Suk Suk*, "*Uncle Stiff Corpse*", a.k.a. **MR. VAM-PIRE SAGA**)
Hong Kong, 1988. D: Ricky Lau Koon-wai
P: Sammo Hung Kam-bo
Cast: Wu Ma, Anthony Chan Yau, Loletta Lee Lai-chun, Yuen Wah, Chin Kar-lok, Chin Siu-ho

Where is Lam Ching-ying as the undefeatable vampire hunter when you need him? Performing the same role in a rival production, most likely! Wu Ma (the heroic priest of the *Chinese Ghost Story* films) stars as heroic Taoist priest Tat-yau in this film, who is assisted by handsome Chin Kar-lok. Anthony Chan appears as a comedy-relief Buddhist Monk, and the two begin the film as rivals before joining forces to fight the vampires. Lovely Category III starlet Loletta Lee is the beauty in peril, and Yuen Wah (usually seen as the heavy or villain in numerous HK films of this period) entertains as the comedic vampire master.

MR. VAMPIRE 4

Although this is an enjoyable entry in the *Mr. Vampire* series, the film seems a bit tired, and the presence of Lam Ching-ying is badly missed.

MR. VAMPIRE 5

(*Jiang Shi Fan Sheng / Geung Si Faan Sang*, "*Stiff Corpse Turns Live*", a.k.a. **NEW MR. VAMPIRE 1**, a.k.a. **KUNG FU VAMPIRE BUSTER**)
Hong Kong, 1986. D: Billy Chan Wui-ngai
Cast: Chin Siu-ho, Lui Fong, Pauline Wong Siu-fung

MR. VAMPIRE

MR. VAMPIRE 1992

Gone is Lam Ching-ying from the series. In his place is his former assistant Chin Siu-ho as one of a pair of bumblers who happen to become involved in reanimated corpses, hopping vampires, and the beautiful Pauline Wong, while battling a vampire clad in golden robes.

The series seems to be grinding to a definite halt with this entry, which makes little attempt to disguise the threadbare budget and regurgitated plot.

MR. VAMPIRE 1992

(*Xin Jiang Shi Xian Sheng / San Geung Si Sin Sang*, "*New Mr. Stiff Corpse*", a.k.a. **MR. VAMPIRE 5**, a.k.a. **VAMPIRE VS. VAMPIRE**)
Hong Kong, 1992. D: Lam Ching-ying, Lau Ka-wing
Action direction: Siu Tak-foo; P: Yip Wing-cho
Cast: Lam Ching-ying, Ricky Hui Koon-ying, Chin Siu-ho, Sandra Ng Kwun-yu, Billy Lau Nam- kwong

Lam Ching-ying returns as another Taoist priest, but this time he does not have to journey far from his homeland as he deals with all manner of supernatural occurrences. A tree splits, and a beautiful, ghostly woman appears draped in a red cloak; she can also turn into an animated cartoon figure, and terrorizes the cast. A swarm of bats converge upon a Western church and nuns attempt to bar the creature's way with planks as they bite their way through the wood. Finally, a rotting corpse reanimates into a vampire, furiously gulping down blood until he becomes a black-caped Westernized version of a blood-

sucker. What is to blame for all of this horrific nonsense? Try the idea of the ghosts of *aborted fetuses…!*

Co-directed by *Mr. Vampire*-hunter himself, this is an oddly-paced, confusing mélange of spook scenes set in the vampire milieu. While the film is far from being the best in the series, it is undoubtedly an entertaining entry and one that is sure to please HK horror aficionados and fans of strange terror films alike.

For many years hopping vampires were a popular item. There were more than a dozen non-Mr. Vampire style films (even X-rated) and TV shows made in Taiwanese, Korean, Indonesia, and even the Philippines. Some of the oddest titles were the "Child Vampire" entries. These kids' films proved very popular, and there were even Hopping Vampire Child toys, as seen above.

An AFTERNOON'S OBSESSION:
Six films caught one Snowy Weekend... or thereabouts

by Tim Paxton

For those of you who read Monster! *'s sister magazine,* Weng's Chop, *you will no doubt know of my somewhat mystifying obsession with Indian Cinema. I've written about it in every issue of* WC *since the very beginning. I've sat through so many that I even dream about finding rare posters and lost Indian monster movies I have never seen. Nevertheless, there are times when I've had my fill of watching Indian movies. Yes, I know, that sounds insane coming from a guy who will sit through three hours of singing and dancing and monsters in Hindi without subtitles. Nutty, right? Actually, no, it isn't. Imagine watching nothing but Italian genre films and little else (I know a few people who do just that). No matter how much of a Fulci, Argento, or D'Amato fan you may well be, you still have to take a breather. As with Indian movies, I like to tune into something I know little about. That way I can be surprised...be it from wonderment or disappointment. The same can be said of randomly watching unknown films on Netflix.*

With a limited income (spent, no surprise there, on Indian films), my go-to streaming service is Netflix via my Roku. I do this on occasion, usually in the afternoons or early evenings when I have come home from work and I need something to watch. It is essential that I don't have to concentrate on understanding the plot because I don't speak the language, or lack of subtitles. For this article I have incorporated two such sessions into one.

After some browsing I have settled on a list of possible choices. First up are some French films about the undead which I found had merit.

For starters, maybe I should list some of the other productions I suffered through over the past few weeks of this kind of screening. There will always be zombie films to choose from, and some of the titles I will gloss over are **ZOMBIE DIARIES 2** (2011, UK; unredeemable trash which lasted all of fifteen minutes before I switched it off), **BONG OF THE DEAD** (2011, Canada; seriously few laughs throughout what I could stand watching), **ABRAHAM LINCOLN VS. ZOMBIES** (2012, USA; pretty much what I expected, so I wasn't too disappointed), and **ZOMBIE APOCALYPSE: REDEMPTION** (2011, USA; another dull, artless bit of drudgery, this also was shut off after about a half-hour). I found those giant monster films on The SyFy Channel to be more satisfying. Maybe it was the commercial breaks. I'm not sure, but Eric Forsberg's **MEGA PIRANHA** (2010, USA) was far more entertaining than, say, Dan Lantz's **BLOODLUST ZOMBIES** (2011, USA) with its tired chemical spill resurrecting the dead and turning them into...well, the title says it all. I haven't seen *all* the living dead films ever

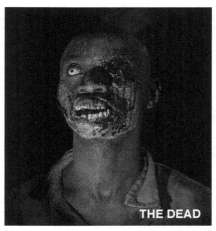

THE DEAD

made, that much is sure. There are a whole lot of American-made productions, as well as those from other countries the world over. I hear that the Indian zombie flick **GO GOA GONE** (2013) is fairly interesting. **THE DEAD** (2010, UK), the one filmed in Africa (not just someone's backyard in California masking as a stand-in for Ghana, etc.), was okay. The plot ambled on a bit and it ended with a very predictable conclusion. I wanted something better than what I saw. I wanted something that would take hold in my psyche and not let go for a while.

I'm dead serious about my zombie films. I love a good one, and really, *really* find the lame, half-assed productions and their attempts at exploiting the flesh-eaters for a quick buck offensive. Not that I am some kind of activist for the rights of the undead, but I want my zombie films to be memorable. **NIGHT OF THE LIVING DEAD**

LA HORDE

(1968, USA), **LIVING DEAD AT THE MAN-CHESTER MORGUE** (*Non si deve profanare il sonno dei morte*, 1974, Italy/Spain), **DAWN OF THE DEAD** (1979, USA), **ZOMBIE** (*Zombi*, 1980, Italy), **NIGHTMARE CITY** (*Incubo sulla città contaminata*, 1980, Italy/Mexico/Spain), **DR. BUTCHER, M.D.** (a.k.a. **ZOMBI HOLOCAUST**, 1980, Italy), **DEAD & BURIED** (1981, USA), and even **RETURN OF THE LIVING DEAD** (1985, USA). All those films had at least five minutes of redeemable material in them. Most are classics. Each added to the lexicon of the undead in their own fashion.

The first film for the afternoon is the 2010 French horror production from directors Yannick Dahan and Benjamin Rocher called **LA HORDE**. The film opens with a police raid gone terribly wrong, and the nightmare spirals out of control and never lets up. A group of rogue officers with personal grudges decide on attacking a small group of drug pushers holed-up in a shitty apartment building somewhere in France. The thugs in the condemned complex murdered a police officer, and a group of the victim's close friends decide to take out the garbage. In what I thought was going to be a nod to Romero's opening scenes of **DAWN OF THE DEAD**, the officers begin advancing through the apartment building looking for the drug smugglers. I half-expected them to open a door to a roomful of flesh-hungry ghouls and unload their hi-powered weaponry into it. The surprise attack doesn't work out as planned, and the officers are instead themselves shot or captured by the criminals.

For no real reason, the dead come back to life, and they thirst for human flesh. This is standard zombie etiquette, I imagine, since most of the post-**NOLD/RETURN OF THE LIVING DEAD** films seem to offer nothing but.[1] What happens next is an exciting romp throughout the building as the remaining cops and robbers team up to dodge the very hungry ghouls/zombies that are after them. Not much is added to the lore of zombiedom within **LA HORDE**, but nevertheless the directors set up some very memorable sequences and allow the characters to be fleshed out somewhat before their ultimate demise. Without giving too much away, the scene where one of the cops is surrounded by hundreds of zombies is handled well, and the final three minutes (while depressing) does makes sense if you take into account the characters and their emotional state.

It doesn't hurt that the lead actress, Claude Perron, resembles a French woman I used to date around 10 years ago. The actress also showed up (albeit briefly) in a few additional wonderful French films, including Jean-Pierre Jeunet's **AMÉLIE** (2001, France/Germany) and Hélène Angel's **RENCONTRE AVEC LE DRAGON** (a.k.a. **THE RED KNIGHT**, 2003, France/Luxembourg). In **LA HORDE**, Perron plays a tough-as-nails female police officer who knows how to handle a gun *and* slug it out with

---

1 If I recall, one of the few such films includes Gary Sherman's superior 1981 chiller **DEAD AND BURIED**, an unsung classic which should be on everyone's zombie bucket list. By the way, it was written by Dan O'Bannon, who wrote and directed **RETURN OF THE LIVING DEAD** (1985).

zombies. She's no withering, wincing female. You gotta love a chick who knows how to fight and carries a big gun. I know I do.

One gripe—albeit a small one—is that no one gets it into their noggins that unloading an automatic weapon into a rampaging zombie's chest and legs isn't the way to kill them (again). Scene after scene when the creatures attack, not one of the characters (who I assume know how to use a gun) took the required head-shot to bring a zombie down. There were some impressive fisticuffs and an effective use of a refrigerator to exterminate a monster, but blasting one in the forehead (as in any Romero film) didn't occur until an undead school teacher was subdued and then taken out with bullet to the brain.

Otherwise **LA HORDE** loped onward at a reasonable clip to its only logical conclusion, with tight camera work, good acting, and only a minimal use of computer-generated gore. And, thankfully, Netflix only had the subtitled version (I have no idea if there is a dubbed version out there, but I find most post-1980s English dubs horrible and unsatisfying—probably because I grew up watching dubbed foreign films on TV or at the drive-ins and got so used to the voice actors who did the dubbing that anything new is just annoying at best).

Whereas **LA HORDE** did borrow the hyperactive virus-infected zombies from **28 DAYS LATER...** (2000, which wasn't the first film to have incredibly fast-moving and ferocious zombies on your tail—check out the aforementioned **NIGHTMARE CITY**) and pretty much used them as a foil for its characters, the next film, David Morlet's **MUTANTS** (2009, France), also had the ultra-fast creatures, but with an added twist. The virus that reanimates the dead also causes the living to become monsters when bitten. Lenzi also explored this somewhat with his film, but not to the degree seen in **MUTANTS**. When I first saw **NIGHTMARE CITY** at our local drive-in (under the moniker **CITY OF THE WALKING DEAD**), I was expecting a Fulcifest of rotten reanimated corpses spewing worms and rot. Nope, Lenzi presented us with humans changing into something else entirely, as does **MUTANTS**. Those infected grow progressively more violent, and at the same time their bodies degenerate into gross and scabby yuckiness. The final transformation has them hunger for human flesh. Lenzi may not have had the budget to get that **MUTANTS** look to his bloodthirsty monsters, but he was on the right track.

As the film opens, there is an ambulance racing along a lonely stretch of road somewhere in France. Inside we have a dying man coughing up

blood, an edgy military officer, and a husband and wife paramedic team. The bloodied man dies and is dragged from the ambulance by the soldier and shot in the head. Later, we begin to learn that some weird virus has taken control of France—maybe even the whole world—and all hell has broken loose. After killing the soldier in a gun battle, our brave couple—the husband mortally wounded—take shelter in an old hospital. Fearing the worst, his wife treats him and hopes for the best...and to their mutual astonishment, his wounds heal overnight. Apparently, the miraculous healing means that he has become infected with the virus. The remainder of the film is about his gradual change into a monster and his wife's problems with him and with other (violent) folks who also take refuge in the building.

MUTANTS is stark and moody, with a (thankfully) minimal musical/weird ambient effects soundtrack and some decent acting. It doesn't hurt that the script is sparse, with the dialogue rather short and curt—giving the actors involved time to stretch their skills between sequences.

As for the monsters in the film, well, I gotta say that they're *okay*. Not the most original-looking creature effects, but much better than, say the similarly bald and hyperactive mutant humans that inhabited Frances Lawrence's horrible 2007 Hollywood version of **I AM LEGEND** (I still insist that the Sidney Salkow/Ubaldo Ragona 1964 version, **THE LAST MAN ON EARTH**, is the best adaptation of the Richard Matheson novel). At least these are monsters created with practical effects and not the cartoony CG deni-

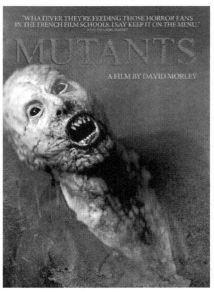

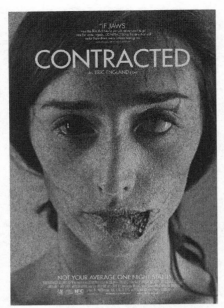

"IF JAWS..."

CONTRACTED
an ERIC ENGLAND film

NOT YOUR AVERAGE ONE NIGHT STAND

IFC

zens that inhabited the Will Smith flick. They are bald, scrappy, have some nasty teeth and weird eyes. *Those* are creature qualities I can live with.

Sometimes you wonder where all this zombie infestation starts. There is the classic form, the pre-**NIGHT OF THE LIVING DEAD** variety, that is by way of a curse or some other magical means. Nowadays, the popular axiom is that the contagion is spread via a bite from one of the undead. Most likely the vector is a virus that somehow reanimates the recently-dead. With Romero's undead this could also be some weird form of radioactive contamination.[2] Sometimes all it takes is a nibble from some mutant rat-monkey, as seen in Peter Jackson's **DEAD ALIVE** (1992). Within the next film, Eric England's **CONTRACTED** (2013), the infection is possibly viral, but the transference is accomplished in a different manner altogether.

As the credits roll we are are witness to an abuse of a female corpse by a morgue attendant. Not much is shown, but the rhythmic squeaking of

[2] There has never been any solid confirmation as to why Romeo's zombies are reanimated. At least, after watching all six of his films, **NIGHT OF THE LIVING DEAD**, **DAWN OF THE DEAD** (1978), **DAY OF THE DEAD** (1985), **LAND OF THE DEAD** (2005), **DIARY OF THE DEAD** (2007), and **SURVIVAL OF THE DEAD** (20009), their form of reanimation has never been fully confirmed. Radiation or chemical exposure were possible (although, again, never confirmed) reasons for the bloodthirsty zombies/infected humans (therefore, monsters) in Umberto Lenzi's **NIGHTMARE CITY**/*Incubo sulla città contaminata* (1980, Italy).

a weight-stressed gurney gives you more than enough information to know that someone is having a bit of "safe" sex. Our mystery man finishes up, replaces the body back in her cooler and leaves.

We are then introduced to Samantha, a young post-grad who is cultivating a rare species of orchid for a show. She is working on keeping her relationship with her mother and girlfriend alive, as her skittish nature leaves much to be desired. Samantha decides to go out for the night to blow off some steam, but unfortunately lands in the middle of a lusty alcohol-fueled party. Once there she is hit on by two of her friends who are really into wanting to sleep with her (kids nowadays…!). After a few drinks—supplied by another girl who wants to bed her—Samantha drunkenly decides on going home with a man who, despite her lesbian conviction and drunken haze, looks like a catch.

The next morning she wakes up, only half understanding that she had sex with someone. Not a big deal, except that it was unprotected intercourse…with a man, not something that her girlfriend Nikki would really be keen on knowing. But something is seriously wrong, as an inordinate amount of blood and goo issues forth from her vagina and her body is covered in a rash. Samantha visits her gynecologist, who insists she contracted some unknown form of STD and urges her to seek further treatment. Soon her condition gets worse, but that doesn't stop her from ignoring that fact that her body is disintegrating. She also has uncontrollable urges that explode into homicidal rage. By the end of the film it's become clear that her necrophilic one-night-stand has given her, and possibly others, a new form of STD. It's not your run-of-the-mill dose of the clap or even herpes…it's a more virulent strain that turns people into, well…*zombies*? I'm not sure about that, as the film ends rather ambiguously, although it's close enough on the edge to be a monster film, so I'll include it in my magazine.

Overall, England's **CONTRACTED** is a satisfying slice of indie film weirdness that reminds me of some low-budget '80s horror production. The acting is surprisingly good, especially from Najarra Townsend, who also starred in Stewart Wade's sexual politics wannabe comedy **TRU LOVED** (2008, Canada) and Michael Ervin's above-average thriller **STRANGE ANGEL** (2010, USA). I would love to see her in more mainstream material other than popping up occasionally on TV shows and as an extra in something like Paul Thomas Anderson's **THE MASTER** (2012, USA).

Time to leave the world of the recently reanimated and into that of the long-dead and vengeful spirit...of a *nun*!

I must admit I have always had a fascination with nuns. Never having grown up Catholic (or even seeing one until I was in college) my only "real" exposure was to a cheerful Sally Fields catching a breeze and soaring through the air on TV's *The Flying Nun* series (1967-70). When I *did* hear the jokes about penguins, rulers and stern looks, none of it made any sense to me. Later, when I dated someone who was Catholic, I heard my first horror stories about some beastly sister and evil mother superiors who treat their young wards with contempt. Later on I found myself enjoying such Nunsploitation classics as Norifumi Suzuki's **SCHOOL OF THE HOLY BEAST** (聖獣学園 / *Seijû gakuen*, 1974, Japan), Juan López Moctezuma's **ALUCARDA** (*Alucarda, la hija de las tinieblas*, 1975, Mexico), and Bruno Mattei's **THE OTHER HELL** (*L'altro inferno*, a.k.a. **GUARDIAN OF HELL**, 1981, Italy). Others followed. Many, *many* films! Once I found out that **THE NUN** (*La monja*, 2005, Spain) was on Netflix, it was a no-brainer.

It is essentially an old-fashioned haunted house film with some modern twists and turns, as a group of women return to the old Catholic school where they spent their childhood. It seems that the sadistic nun Sister Ursula, who tortured them as youths and whom they though was dead, has returned from her watery grave. This unholy spirit (the film would have us believe that all nuns are self-righteous and sadistic in nature; something that is a common overall acceptance in much of the cinematic landscape) picks off her former charges one-by-one. Each woman is killed based on a list of the convent's martyrs, and how they met their particular demise. Can the remaining women make it out of the old nunnery alive?

THE NUN was directed by Spanish filmmaker Luis de la Madrid, who cut his teeth as editor for Jaume Balagueró's spooky-as-shit **THE NAMELESS** (*Los sin nombre*, 1999, Spain), and other Spanish-shot items including Brian Yunza's funky **FAUST** (2000), Guillermo del Toro's scary ghost thriller **THE DEVIL'S BACKBONE** (*El espinazo del diablo*, 2001)—a coproduction between Spain, Mexico and Argentina—and Brad Anderson's **THE MACHINIST** (2004) before tackling his own demons with **THE NUN**, his only feature-length outing. As productions go, the film has moments of spookiness as the vicious water-borne spirit rises out of tubs, faucets, shower heads, etc. The film moves along at a nice clip despite the milquetoast actors

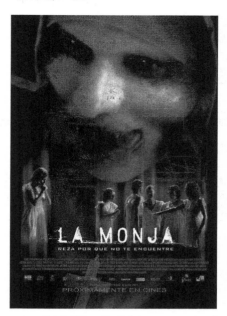

and a cliché-ridden English-language script. I wonder, had the film been in Spanish rather than with English-speaking actors, might the end result have been tighter and more believable? Hard to tell.

As far as ghost lore goes, the film covers a lot of ground and does so with the logic usually associated with hauntings. The ending, which I

EMBRACE YOUR
INNER DEMON.

MAGNOLIA PICTURES and NEW ARTISTS ALLIANCE present a DUPLASS BROTHERS PRODUCTION
in association with FLOREN SHIEH PRODUCTIONS

BAD MILO!

KEN MARINO · GILLIAN JACOBS · PATRICK WARBURTON · MARY KAY PLACE and STEPHEN ROOT and PETER STORMARE

IT'S COMING OUT THIS FALL

is one of the very first SF films and features crustacean-like monsters (something also seen in the Ray Harryahusen flick **FIRST MEN IN THE MOON** [1964, UK]). Moon maidens and giant spiders appeared in Richard E. Cunha's **MISSLE TO THE MOON** (1958, USA), and a weird mechanical alien life-form causes trouble for Bruce Campbell and Walter Koenig in Robert Dyke's entertaining **MOONTRAP** (1986, USA). In the case of **APOLLO 18**, the monsters are able to infest their human hosts and take command of their higher functions. Apparently, these things are stuck on the moon (their ship crashed eons ago?), and they need us to get them off that barren rock to someplace more hospitable (at least that's what I got from the film). Hijacking humans seems to do the trick, and when the crew of an earlier Soviet manned ship didn't serve their purpose, these things go after our two red-blooded American astronauts.

To say the least, I really enjoyed the film, and this is coming from a self-confirmed Apollo junkie who used to collect tapes of NASA audio chatter, and who regularly listens to the SomaFM streaming channel *Mission Control* (which features a mix of ambient and experimental music mixed with the historical sounds of the space program).

As far as the director of the film goes, López-Gallego was also responsible for the Spanish-language film **NÓMADAS** (2001), which I've never seen, but by all reports is supposed to be very good.

"I had a monster *up my ass, it is the furthest thing from a metaphor!"*

How many of you remember the '80s TV show *Monsters*? It was an anthology series from producer Richard P. Rubinstein, who brought the world *Tales from the Darkside*. As independent TV programming went, *Monsters* was better than most. It had a minimal budget, which kept their effects on a primitive level, but nevertheless, as with its predecessor, the scripts helped matters immensely. Now, imagine one of its wackier episodes made into a full-length film and you have **BAD MILO** (2013, USA, D: Jacob Vaughan).

The premise is plain and simple: Duncan is an anxious, overstressed man who has an Aztec demon living in his digestive tract. As his life at work becomes unbearable and he is at his breaking point, the monster in Duncan's butt senses his host's anxiety, and like any good symbiotic parasite takes action to assure its survival. Duncan has a particularly bad day at the office, and comes home feeling horrible. He passes out on

won't give away, is fairly cool. Most of the effects in the film are your usual spotty mid-2000s low-budget CGI, but Madrid's tight editing keeps these sparse spectral frights from being all-too-obvious.

Day Two of my monster marathon, with a stab at my least-favorite subgenre of horror film these days: the found footage ("FF") scenario.

As found footage films go, I rather thought my first choice for this afternoon's viewing was fairly good. The premise behind Gonzalo López-Gallego's **APOLLO 18** (2011, USA/Canada) is that what you are watching is recently uncovered 16 or 32mm film footage from a clandestine mission to the moon. We are witness to the Apollo 18 mission, which was the very last *unofficial* manned landing. As cool as I find space travel films, I wouldn't have included it in *Monster!* if it didn't feature some sort of alien critter. In this case the monsters are (possibly) intelligent crab-like things. These scuttling horrors can mimic moon rocks, and thus were able to gain entrance to the lunar landing module. Not unlike in a Quatermass film, these things apparently have an ulterior motive, but whatever their plans are for the Earth is unclear.

As plots go, **APOLLO 18** is your garden variety man-lands-on-the-moon-and-is-attacked-by-some-unknown-life-form movie. Other movies in this genre have included Georges Méliès' **A TRIP TO THE MOON** (1902, France), which

the toilet, and the demon crawls out of his anus. The creature, which resembles a baby-sized goblin, then goes on a search-and-destroy mission to ease his host's suffering. After a few instances of pain, passing out, and later hearing about the bloody demise of his co-workers, etc., Duncan begins to suspect something is seriously wrong and consults a doctor (the amazing Peter Stormare), and together they are able to manifest the demon (a.k.a. Milo) so that Duncan can deal with it directly. Apparently, this possession/condition is hereditary, and Duncan must hunt down his estranged father (Stephen Root—you gotta love him!) for a possible remedy.

What is surprising about **BAD MILO** is that there are very few poop jokes. The film is well-written and -directed, and features a stellar cast, and Milo is, for the most part, a practical effects puppet rather than some CG-created creature (although there is some computer tweaking here and there). That is not to say I dislike CG, but in a film like this one I love to see animatronic/puppet critters. In the case of **BAD MILO**, the puppeteers were Frank Langley and Bob Mano, the two talented guys who worked on the ultimate post-Gerry Anderson film **TEAM AMERICA** (2004, USA, D: Trey Parker). Think of this ass-demon as a muppet gone bad...maybe Cookie Monster when he was told he had to only eat veggies from now on. It may not be a film for everyone, but this monster fan enjoyed it immensely.

Oh, and as a happy side note: *Monsters* finally got a DVD release through Entertainment One in February of this year. All 72 episodes on nine discs. Sweet.

What began as a weekend afternoon zombiefest soon expanded into a total monster movie marathon. A general spiraling-out from the living dead into all sorts of territory. The final film of the festival was more along the lines of what I was used to watching when drive-in theaters were commonplace in America. **STORAGE 24** (2012, UK) was released theatrically in the USA in 2013, and I've been told that it was the biggest bomb of the year.[3] But then again, **STORAGE 24** was a small British film with no real potentially bankable star, released with little fanfare. I found out about it only recently, and that was during one of my Netflix random picks.

The plot is a fairly straightforward cat-and-mouse monster-stalking movie. Not much has

changed since the early days of Christian Nyby/ Howard Hawks' **THE THING** (1951) or Edward L. Cahn/Jerome Bixby's **IT! THE TERROR FROM BEYOND SPACE** (1958)—a claustrophobic classic probably better-known now for its many similarities to Ridley Scott's **ALIEN** (1979, USA/UK)—wherein a monstrous Martian stows away on a spaceship bound for Earth. That narrative has been a popular one for over 60 years, be it on an isolated arctic station, a ship deep in space...or in a storage lockup in the middle of London.

The film begins with a break-up; girl dumps boy in the worst way possible. This one is particularly bad: (ex-) girlfriend moves all your stuff out of the apartment you shared to an offsite storage facility. She does it with the help of your best friend, who is the reason for the break-up. You, her and the new lover all meet at the said storage location for a final confrontation...what could be worse? Oh yeah, there's a monster in the building. That sucks. That set-up admittedly sounds dumb, and it is if you care to sit down and try to suss-out all the details. But who wants to do that when you can simply have fun with a monster-on-the-loose flick like this one?

The boyfriend, Charlie (Noel Clark), and his best mate Mark (Colin O'Donoghue) are on their way to find out where his ex-girlfriend Shelley (Antonia Campbell-Hughes) and her friends Nikki and Chris have stashed their belongings. The duo end up at a storage complex in the middle of London, where they and some other people become trapped when a weird power outage shuts the building down (the security system automatically drops down metal gates and locks all the doors if there is an emergency). Sadly, there is no way to get the exits open again until the power comes back on... and there is something not quite human in the complex with them.

Tempers flare as Charlie realizes that Shelly has been sleeping with Mark, but all that takes a back seat when the monster—a grotesque knob-

BAD MILO

3 Gander, Kashmira, "Lowest-grossing movie of 2013: British-made Storage 24 brings in $72 at US box office", The Independent (*independent.co.uk*), January 8, 2014.

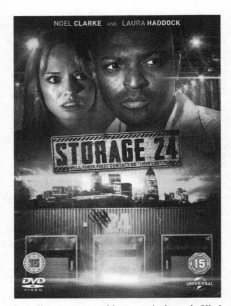

by/spiky creature with a vertical tooth-filled maw and long sharp claws—begins to slash and tear its way through the cast.

Clark, a familiar face to the fans of the rebooted *Doctor Who* franchise, has been slowly making his way up the ladder of UK stardom since the early '90s. Recently he starred in Neil Marshall's **CENTURION** (2010, UK/France), J.J. Abrams' **STAR TREK INTO DARKNESS** (2013, USA), and Ronnie Thompson's **I AM SOLDIER** (2014, UK). I like this actor, and was very happy to see him in **STORAGE 24**. His involvement in the film also included the story for the screenplay...which may not have been a major achievement for him, but I'm a sucker for

any monster film which reminds me of an old Tom Baker *Doctor Who* episode.

And the creature that does the munching? It's mostly of practical design. That is, there is some CG in the film, but most of the scenes with the monster consist of good old-fashioned rubbery goodness. Whereas **BAD MILO**'s little butt demon was played for laughs and was cool in the way that Belial was portrayed in Frank Henelotter's *Basket Case* films (1982-1991, USA), the **STORAGE 24** monster is a wonderfully-designed full-suit endeavor, for the most part. That said, I have no complaints about the film—except for the final few minutes, which was less than original and opened everything up for a sequel. I don't see that happening, though.

So, all in all, this two-day afternoon-to-evening adventure paid off. I watched some pretty good monster flicks and my head is now clear for jumping back into my sub-continental obsession. One thing I have noticed after all of this is how vastly different monster movies are in India and the West. It's hard to quantify, but it is a totally different mindset. From what I have seen, when it comes to Indian monster movies (and I have watched literally hundreds of that country's horror/monster/musical mash-ups), it is exceptionally rare for there to be a 100% creature feature that's truly satisfying. Typically you will have to sit through a lot of crap to get to the good bits. There are exceptions, and I will give you one example just because little has been written about the film.

Last year in one of my random buying binges I decided to get a few films that looked like they could be monster movies. I usually purchase 15-20 films at a time to save on shipping, and for the most part the good-versus-bad ratio of film

STORAGE 24

content is very low, and I end up with a lot of so-so wannabe horror films. In this pile I had a few okay ones, including Louis Wilson's **KAALO** (2011) and the Haresh Narayan/K. Hari Shankar co-directed film **AMBULI** (2012).

KAALO I reviewed for *Monster!*'s sister publication *Weng's Chop*, and I will give it a brief mention a little later on. But I had high hopes for the Tamil horror film **AMBULI**. It was originally made in stereoscopic 3D, a first for any Tamil film. My DVD was 2D, which was okay by me. The DVD art for the film was old-school, showing a large clawed hand dripping with blood. The film's poster makes the critter out to be the little brother of the alien from **PREDATOR** (1987) with its dreads (or possibly like that of the Hindu god Shiva? Naw, more likely the Stan Wilson creation!)

As with the majority of Indian films I have covered, this DVD doesn't have English subtitles, but it seems that decades ago a woman gave birth to monstrous baby and the mysterious "Sir Wellington College of Arts and Science" has a connection to its existence.

As with Larry Cohen's **IT'S ALIVE** (1974, USA), the creature can kill from the moment it's delivered into our world (as shown in some cartoony flashbacks; we see the monster demolish a few folk and then escape into a millet field). Apparently it has lived in this field for years, occasionally snacking on both people and animals. Two college kids stumble onto the village's monstrous secret. Soon after the creature was born and escaped, a wall was erected to enclose the monster within the boundaries of the college and its estate.

The film looks pretty good for what it is, and that says a lot, since the aforementioned **KAALO** was such a major disappointment. In that film we are treated to a hideous witch that devours children and traps a busload of vacationers for easy picking. At least **AMBULI** doesn't suffer from "I am a cool guy director who thinks he's Guy Ritchie" syndrome that plagued the look and pace of **KAALO**. Like **STORAGE 24**, **AMBULI** is a throwback to Indie drive-in fare I grew up on. The film does get rather talky at times, but then again most Indian films are blabfests. There are a few required musical numbers, and, thankfully, a monster. If you want to compare the two films further, **KAALO** and **AMBULI** are both folklore-based horrors, albeit the directors of the Tamil film do inject some elements of SF into the backstory of their film's creature. It is less a supernatural monster like the flying witch from Wilson's film, and more of something borrowed from H.G. Wells.

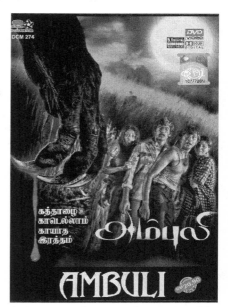

As it turns out, the monster is a creation of the old headmaster of the college. In 1947, the English-born founder of the college, Sir Wellington, a guy who liked to dabble in science, gets his hands on some "Neanderthal extract" (I *think* that's what was said in the film). With nothing else to do, he then experiments with this "extract" on a local village woman who is having a difficult pregnancy (oh, no racism here, folks!). On the night of the child's birth, which happens to be on the date of a lunar eclipse, the superhuman/Neanderthal hybrid is somehow affected by "lunar radiation". The child turns into a some-

thing nonhuman, and our headmaster got hisself a monster. The unfortunate child is named Ambuli, which means "moon" in Tamil. The film bogs down a bit towards the middle, but things begin to pick up after a few musical numbers are over and done with. It's been 90 minutes, and I still haven't had a good glimpse of the thing. I'm twiddling my thumbs waiting for Ambuli to show (at this point **KAALO** is starting to look better and better; at least you got to see the monster fairly frequently, even though the horrible CG effects and arty cinematography made it cringeworthy). But I'm cheering for **AMBULI**.

JAANI DUSHMAN

Waiting for the payoff...

The three students and the caretaker of the millet field track the creature to the ruins of an old underground temple (shades of Rajkumar Kohli's groundbreaking Indian monster flick **JAANI DUSHMAN** [1979]), where it turns out that Ambuli is a gorilla like ape-man. *And*, I am very happy to report that he's also a good ol'-fashioned fur-covered rubber monster! Thank god, I was afraid it would be CG. We see a lot of the monster when there's an extended battle between Ambuli and some of those meddling kids. Just before our monster is about to snack on the humans, an army helicopter and men with tranquilizer guns emerge, confront, and captures the beast. You see, this superhuman creature is just what the army ordered for its new Super Soldier program.

Oh yes, I'm expecting a sequel any day now. Bring it on, because I'm running low on stuff to watch on Netflix.

AMBULI

LOTUS FIVESTAR DVD

64

MONSTER! #4 MOVIE CHECKLIST

MONSTER! Public Service posting: Title availability of films reviewed or mentioned in this issue of MONSTER!
Information dug up and presented by Steve Fenton and Tim Paxton.

AMBULI – Formerly available on disc, but now OOP. There is a truly atrocious rip upped to You-Tube in several parts (evidently sneaky-cammed from a cinema screen in some fleapit on the subcontinent somewhere), but don't waste your time; although there is a pretty decent quality widescreen trailer up there too, for those interested in a taster of what to expect. If you can't turn up a copy any other way (give *induna.com* or *myindiashopping.com* a try), there's always the torrent site route, so why not give Vuze a shot...

ANAK NG BULKAN – Ripped from an airing on an indeterminate date on commercial Pinoy TV and uploaded in 8 separate parts, the far from good if by no means unwatchable copy on YouTube is further marred by having distracting watermarks plastered all over it throughout, but with a movie this rare and exotic, we gotta be happy with what we can get. Apparently, the original prints of many Filipino films from the period in which it was made (pre-1960) have since become lost, so we can't be too choosy. Despite the far less than ideal condition of the version I watched—which is presumably one of the very few (TV?) prints still in any sort of circulation—we can be thankful that someone was good enough to upload it in at least some form. So try to ignore the at times heavily pockmarked print and atrocious, surface noise-laden audio track and just enjoy the film, OK? Thanks to Tim P. for bringing this movie to my attention. Until he told me about it, I never even knew it existed! I'm pretty sure Cirio H. Santiago's schmaltzed-up '97 "reboot" of the same name is way easier to come by, but I doubt it'll be anywhere near as good.

APOLLO 18 – Available on NTSC Region 1 Blu-ray and DVD from The Weinstein Company. It was also made available in the same formats from the same company in an All-Region version, in English with French subs. There is a quite decent-looking unauthorized upload of it viewable / downloadable free of charge on You-Tube, or you can cough-up $14.99 and purchase a copy via the same site. Your choice. Which option are *you* gonna choose…?

BAD MILO – Available on NTSC Region 1 Blu-ray and DVD from Magnolia Home Entertainment / Magnet.

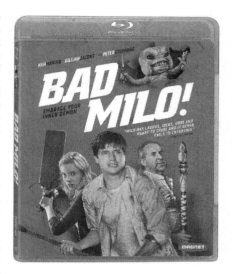

BIGFOOT AT HOLLER CREEK CANYON – Not that I tried too hard, I must confess, but I couldn't rustle-up any disc info on this title, which appears to be about as elusive as the title critter itself. But it's out there somewhere, so keep your eyes peeled for a sighting. Only don't blame *Monster!* if it turns out to be just some dude in a cheap gorilla-suit, OK?

BIGFOOT'S WILD WEEKEND – Couldn't for the life of me find a listing for a disc of this online either, but, quite frankly, I wasn't gonna waste too much time looking. It is up for grabs for a mere (!) $9.99 (!!) on YouTube, but from the looks of the trailer, I'll pass. Even for 99¢, it'd be 98¢ too much! (And *no*, I'm not a bigfoot bigot, OK! ☺)

CONTRACTED – Available in the USA and Canada on NTSC Region 1 Blu-ray and DVD from MPI Home Video.

EROTIC GHOST STORY 1-3 – The entire loose trilogy has at some point been made available as separate All-Region DVDs by Universe Laser & Video Co. of Hong Kong, as well as in any number of other incarnations internationally as well. I scored English-subbed "grey market" (i.e., Triad bootleg) copies of all three films on

tles in the franchise have also been released on Region 1 DVD by various companies, including Platinum Disc (**HOWLING IV: THE ORIGINAL NIGHTMARE**) and Anchor Bay (**THE HOWLING REBORN**).

INCIDENT AT LOCH NESS – Available on NTSC Region 1 Blu-ray and DVD from 20th Century-Fox Home Video.

KAALO – Issued as an All-Region DVD in the NTSC format by Beyond Dreams Entertainment, and available from the Induna website (*induna. com*). For those interested, there is (*was?*) a really sharp, hi-rez 720p widescreen copy—complete with English subs, yet (*bonus!*)—uploaded to YouTube at the link entitled *Kalo - The Witch of the Desert*.

LA HORDE – Available English-dubbed on NTSC Region 1 Blu-ray and DVD from Alliance Canada. It is also available in the same two formats from IFC Independent Film, in the original French with English subs.

MR. VAMPIRE 1-5 – While the series has been issued in innumerable versions of multiple formats over the years since they were first released to home videocassette way back shortly following their theatrical runs, the best bet to source copies in more recent years would likely be through the Fortune Star company, who put out the entire (?) series—or at the very least the first four (?) of the films on DVD, typically in their original Chinese versions with foreign subs (English included), but I do believe some of the series might have been dubbed into English and other languages too. There are about a trillion uploads of the *Mr. Vampire* flicks on YT in assorted formats, so by all means have a browse around there and take your pick…if you can tell one from the other! In addition to Louis Paul's reviews in this ish, by all means check out fellow *Monster!* alumnus Brian Harris' in-depth article on the subject—entitled "Jiangshi Journals: Ricky Lau & the Five Misters"—in *Weng's Chop* #5 (howzat for a subtle plug for our sexy sister 'zine, eh?!).

MR. VAMPIRE 1992 – Formerly available on Hong Kong DVD in Chinese (possibly with English subs) from Thunder Media. It was evidently also once extant in the same format from HK's Chinastar company. Any version is now apparently as rare as *jiangshi* teeth, so if you find one, hop to it (*sorry*). I'm at least 90% positive it's on YouTube, but I already have a decent download of it from a torrent site, so I'll leave

DVD real cheap (about $2 a pop!) in Toronto's Chinatown some years back. Possibly there might be a legit box set floating around by now? Just a guess.

EROTIC GHOST STORY: PERFECT MATCH – Available on All-Region Hong Kong DVD from Tai Seng Entertainment, in Chinese with English subs; the same company also released it in the same form on VHS videocassette. I picked up a pirate copy in Toronto's Chinatown, which, as I recall (I haven't checked) came complete with English subs… who knows, they might actually have been quite intelligible too, for all I know. So you pays your money and you takes your chances.

GORGO – Available on NTSC Region 1 Blu-ray and DVD from VCI Entertainment.

THE HOWLING (Collector's Edition) – Available on NTSC Region 1 Blu-ray and DVD from Shout! Factory. In conjunction with Timeless Media, in 2009 the same company has also released the film as part of the *Howling Trilogy*; a deluxe-packaged edition of the first 3 films in the series, which came in a decorative tin, loaded with extra features. Back in 2003, Metro-Goldwyn-Mayer Home Video released **THE HOWLING** in a "Special Edition" DVD, Region 1 NTSC format; in 2010, MGM also put it out as a double feature disc co-billed with the notorious first sequel **HOWLING II: YOUR SISTER IS A WEREWOLF**. Various other tiit to you to do a search for it at YT: due to all the other *Mr. Vampire* franchise entries (both Ricky Lau's official ones and all the many rip-offs) being up there and because there is such a maze of misinformation and mix-ups surrounding the films, good luck finding the present title (which is sometimes for some reason confused with 1986's **NEW MR. VAMPIRE**, a non-Lau entry). As for the present film, I originally saw it aired on Halloween Night 1993—double-billed with Sammo Hung's kickass **ENCOUNTER OF THE SPOOKY KIND II**—on Toronto multilingual TV (CFMT Channel 47, Cable 4); for which airing a scene showing infantile urination and one of a little boy getting his teensy tallywhacker stretched like a rubber band (*T-W-A-A-A-N-G-G-G!*) was censored. For those who just *have* to see that, uncut prints are available. I can still remember a great surreal subtitle from the print I watched all the way back in '93: "It's akin, it's very akin". Quite.

THE MUD MONSTER – At some point released on Region 1 DVD by Cinefear. The copy available for viewing at YouTube is exceedingly muddy (pun intended!), but whaddaya want for free?! I couldn't find it up for sale at Amazon, but apparently it is/was available via the *superstrangevideo.com* website.

MUTANTS – Available on NTSC Region 1 Bluray and DVD from MPI Home Video.

THE NUN – Available on NTSC Region 1 DVD from Lions Gate Entertainment, with English dialogue and optional Spanish subs.

PURANA MANDIR – Double-billed with **BANDH DARWAZA** (reviewed in *Monster!* #3), this was formerly available (now OOP) on full-frame Region 1 DVD from Mondo Macabro, in Hindi with English subs.

PURANI HAVELI: MANSION OF EVIL – Double-billed with **VEERANA: VENGEANCE OF THE VAMPIRE**, this was formerly available (now OOP) on full-frame Region 1 DVD from Mondo Macabro, in Hindi with English subs. It also orderable on domestic Indian VCD and DVD from Induna (*induna.com*).

THE RIFT* – Under the title **ENDLESS DESCENT**, this was formerly available on N. American VHS/Beta tape and laserdisc from LIVE Home Video (*circa* the '90s). It was also released in the Netherlands by RCA/Columbia Home Video, possibly (?) in English with Dutch subs. The apparently widescreen version I downloaded from a torrent site via Vuze may

only have been matted so as to appear to be in the widescreen format, as an MGM logo watermark is clearly visible in the lower right-hand corner of the frame, partially cropped-off by the black matting strip at the bottom of the screen. There's an upload—see: *The Rift (aka Endless Descent, 1990) - DSRip*—at Kickass Torrents (*kickass. to*), but it appears to be a dead torrent, with no seeders. Check out these choice excerpts from the narration to the US video trailer (which is up for view on YouTube): *"Where DEEPSTAR SIX left off, ENDLESS DESCENT begins... an endless descent into HELL! With special effects by the creators of ALIEN... ENDLESS DESCENT: it will take you to the very depths of TERROR!"* If you want a taster that's even more mouth-watering than that aforc-quoted trailer, click on the following link at YT: *Endless Descent - The Rift (Montage of Monsters)*; it conveniently condenses most of the coolest scenes into a single 3½-minute chunk of deliciously monstrous madness. The full movie is also up there, albeit only in Spanish (click on *La Grieta (1990) [Completa]*). I seem to remember checking a month or two back, and there was a rip of the full English-language LIVE videotape version on YT as well, but if it was it seems to have disappeared now. Those who really wanna see this thing badly enough should be able to turn up a user-friendly copy from somewhere without too much difficulty. For instance, via Amazon instant video, it can be rented or purchased for $2.99 and $9.99 respectively. They also offer a brand-new Japanese NTSC All-Region DVD (label unnamed) of

YOU CAN'T HOLD YOUR BREATH AND SCREAM AT THE SAME TIME

endless descent

DVD

the film—presented full-frame, in English, with Japanese subs—for a mere *$200.29* (!?); hopefully for that price it at least comes in the original shrink-wrap! Most of the customer reviews at Amazon are, to put it mildly, less than flattering towards the film (e.g., *"Whew! Really?"*). *Not to be confused with **THE RIFT**, a short (25m) alien invasion film from 2012; directed by Robert Kouba, it boasts some pretty damn impressive CG FX for an SOV indy production, and is well worth a watch.

ROMANCE OF THE VAMPIRES – Available on (All-Region?) DVD from Ocean Shores Video Ltd., in the original Chinese with English subs.

SHRIEK OF THE SASQUATCH – Available on full-frame NTSC Region 1 DVD from Retro-Media. Judging by the cover art, here's a bigfoot flick I can finally get behind! BTW, about those BF movie disses I made above and below: don't take my word for it, I haven't seen any of the buggers other than for a trailer and a few clips, whereas in this very ish Douglas Waltz has diligently watched all 4 of the assorted 'foot and 'squatch movies listed here, so he's far better able to judge than I am… but of course, personal opinions are entirely subjective, after all.

STORAGE 24 – Available English-dubbed on NTSC Region 1 Blu-ray from Magnolia Home Entertainment / Magnet. Also available in the UK on Region 2 Blu-ray and DVD from Universal Pictures. Various other English-language,

foreign-subbed disc versions are available worldwide.

SUBURBAN SASQUATCH – Trust me, you really don't need to see this rot! (I scanned through a few clips on YT, and that was plenty: *too much*, in fact.) But if you insist on subjecting yourself to such masochistic torture, it's available on NTSC Region 1 DVD from Troubled Moon Films… God only knows why! ☺

TO KAKO – Under the title **EVIL**, this is available on NTSC Region 1 Blu-ray and DVD from Danger After Dark, in the original Greek with English subs. I'm sure it's alternately available via any number of other sources too.

TO KAKO 2 (TO KAKO - STIN EPOHI TON IROON) – As **EVIL: IN THE TIME OF HEROES**, this is up for grabs as an Amazon instant video, and can be rented for $2.99 or purchased for $9.99; it was released on DVD (and presumably Blu too) by Doppelgänger Releasing, in the original Greek with English subs. It can also be streamed at a number of sites online. Give Netflix a shot.

THE VAMPIRE OF THE OPERA – Originally titled **IL MOSTRO DELL'OPERA** in Italy and for France **L'ORGIE DES VAMPIRES** (can you guess what that translates to, boys and girls? I thought so!), this is available on Region 2 PAL DVD from Artus Films, in the original Italian with English and French subs. For a mere 99¢ a pop at Amazon (*http://www.amazon.com/ Il-mostro-dellopera-Aldo-Piga/dp/B00CVS-GTEU*), soundtrack enthusiasts can download all 15 tracks from Aldo Piga's original score, released on the Creazioni Artistiche Musicali C.A.M. S.r.l. label; but if you ask me, a penny short of a buck is pretty steep for a tune of a mere 1:11 minutes duration! But most of the rest of the cuts are quite a bit longer, so it all evens out, I suppose.

VISIT TO HELL – I could find no video sources for this film in any format under either the present title or its alternate Anglo title, **VISA TO HELL**; which isn't to say it doesn't exist on disc in some form (VCD maybe?); but other than that, I dunno what to tell ya, peeps.

69

40206242R00044

Made in the USA
Lexington, KY
31 March 2015